A Guide
to
Virtual Private Networks

ISBN 0-13-083964-7

90000

9 780130 839640

The ITSO Networking Series

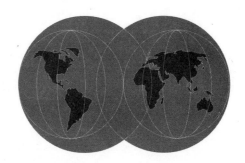

A Guide to Virtual Private Networks
   by Murhammer, Bourne, Gaidosch, Kunzinger, Rademacher, and Weinfurter

TCP/IP Tutorial and Technical Overview, Sixth Edition
   by Murhammer, Atakan, Bretz, Pugh, Suzuki, and Wood

Understanding Optical Communications
   by Dutton

Asynchronous Transfer Mode (ATM)
   by Dutton and Lenhard

High-Speed Networking Technology
   by Dutton and Lenhard

www.security: How to Build a Secure World Wide Web Connection
   by Macgregor, Aresi, and Siegert

Internetworking over ATM: An Introduction
   by Dorling, Freedman, Metz, and Burger

Inside APPN and HPR
   by Dorling, Lenhard, Lennon, and Uskokovic

JAVA™ Network Security
   by Macgregor, Durbin, Owlett, and Yeomans

A Guide to
Virtual Private Networks

MARTIN W. MURHAMMER ■ TIM A. BOURNE ■
TAMAS GAIDOSCH ■ CHARLES KUNZINGER ■
LAURA RADEMACHER ■ ANDREAS WEINFURTER

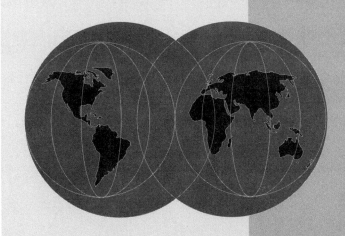

PRENTICE HALL PTR, UPPER SADDLE RIVER, NEW JERSEY 07458
http://www.phptr.com

For information about redbooks:
http://www.redbooks.ibm.com

Send comments to:
redbooks@us.ibm.com

Published by Prentice Hall PTR
Prentice-Hall, Inc.
Upper Saddle River, NJ 07458

Prentice Hall books are widely used by corporations and government agencies for training, marketing, and resale. The publisher offers discounts on this book when ordered in bulk quantities. For more information, contact

        Corporate Sales Department,
        Phone 800-382-3419; FAX: 201-236-7141
        E-mail (Internet): corpsales@prenhall.com

Or Write: Prentice Hall PTR
        Corporate Sales Department
        One Lake Street
        Upper Saddle River, NJ 07458

Take Note! Before using this information and the product it supports, be sure to read the general information under Appendix C, "Special Notices" on page 153.

Printed in the United States of America
10 9 8 7 6 5 4 3 2 1

ISBN   0-13-083964-7

Prentice-Hall International (UK) Limited, *London*
Prentice-Hall of Australia Pty. Limited, *Sydney*
Prentice-Hall Canada Inc., *Toronto*
Prentice-Hall Hispanoamericana, S.A., *Mexico*
Prentice-Hall of India Private Limited, *New Delhi*
Prentice-Hall of Japan, Inc., *Tokyo*
Simon & Schuster Asia Pte. Ltd., *Singapore*
Editora Prentice-Hall do Brasil, Ltda., *Rio de Janeiro*

Contents

Figures

Tables

Preface

This book describes how to implement virtual private networks (VPNs) based on authentication, encryption, and the exchange of security keys, as defined in the IP Security Architecture (IPSec) standard and draft documents.

This book will help readers to identify the benefits of VPNs and then to successfully deploy VPNs. The most commonly used encryption algorithms and handshaking protocols are explained as a general introduction to IP security.

Scenarios describe how to set up IP tunnelling via existing IP networks and the Internet to effectively implement secure and private conversations over public networks. The sceanrios illustrate point-to-point (client-to-server, server-to-server or client-to-client), branch office (LAN-LAN) and remote user (client-LAN) environments.

An outlook is provided on further development in this area, including certificate and key management frameworks such as Internet Key Exchange (IKE), formerly referred to as ISAKMP/Oakley.

This book essentially presents a subset of the information contained in the IBM redbook *A Comprehensive Guide to Virtual Private Networks, Volume I: IBM Firewall, Server and Client Solutions*, June 1998, IBM publication number SG24-5201, but also contains updated information according to the latest IPSec standards.

The Authors

This publication was produced by a team of specialists from around the world working at the International Technical Support Organization Raleigh Center. The leader of this project was Martin W. Murhammer.

Martin W. Murhammer is a Senior I/T Availability Professional at the International Technical Support Organization Raleigh Center. Before joining the ITSO in 1996, he was a Systems Engineer in the Systems Service Center at IBM Austria. He has 13 years of experience in the personal computing environment including such areas as heterogeneous connectivity, server design, system recovery, and Internet solutions. He is a Certified OS/2 Engineer and a Certified LAN Server Engineer and has previously coauthored six redbooks during residencies at the ITSO Raleigh and Austin Centers.

Tim A. Bourne is an Advisory Software Engineer at the IBM PC Company. He has 10 years of experience in software design and development including implementation of Internet protocols, air traffic control and embedded communication systems.

Tamas Gaidosch is an I/T Architect in IBM Hungary. He specializes in networking software and e-business solutions in the banking industry. Tamas has five years of experience in networked computing environments and systems administration. He holds a Master's degree in Computer Science. His areas of expertise include operating systems (OS/2 LAN Server, Windows NT, AIX), networks (TCP/IP, X.25) and self-service banking software.

Charles Kunzinger is a Senior Engineer in Research Triangle Park, with responsibility for the technical integrity of IBM's Virtual Private Network line of products. He has worked for IBM since 1967 in various development, advanced technology, and architecture groups. For the last ten years, he has had extensive experience in the development of network layer open standards, and has represented IBM in various open standards bodies, covering such areas as interdomain routing, mobile-IP, and wireless communications, and has contributed to the development of open security standards in each of these fields.

Laura Rademacher is a member of the VPN Brand Management group located in Research Triangle Park, NC, and has spent much of her marketing career on the promotion of VPN technology and solutions. Prior to joining the marketing organization, she was in the TCP/IP technology area, focusing her time mainly on the education and advancement of Internet security. Laura has 15 years of experience with IBM.

Andreas Weinfurter is an Advisory I/T Availability Professional at the IBM System Services Center in Salzburg, Austria. After joining IBM in 1988 he worked as an instructor at the IBM education center in Vienna, where he was responsible for the PC curriculum and held mainly classes on OS/2 and networking. His primary areas of work for the past six years have been AIX and TCP/IP with a strong focus on firewalls during the last two years. Andreas holds a Master's degree in Computer Science from the Vienna University of Technology.

Thanks to the following people for their invaluable contributions to this project:

Tim Kearby, Karl Wozabal, Jorge Ferrari, Margaret Ticknor
Shawn Walsh, Kathryn Casamento, Linda Robinson
International Technical Support Organization Raleigh Center

Bob Tunstall, Vach Kompella, Jaime Claypool, Steven Lingafelt
Linwood Overby, Cindy Stone-Rutherford
IBM Research Triangle Park

Jackie Wilson, Chris Wenzel, Shay Hoffmaster
IBM Austin

Richard Planutis
IBM Endicott

Chapter 1. Virtual Private Networks (VPN) Overview

The Internet has become a popular, low-cost backbone infrastructure. Its universal reach has led many companies to consider constructing a secure virtual private network (VPN) over the public Internet. The challenge in designing a VPN for today's global business environment will be to exploit the public Internet backbone for both intra-company and inter-company communication while still providing the security of the traditional private, self-administered corporate network.

In this chapter, we begin by defining a virtual private network (VPN) and explaining the benefits that customers can achieve from its implementation. After discussing the security considerations and planning aspects, we then describe the VPN solutions available in the market today.

1.1 VPN Introduction and Benefits

With the explosive growth of the Internet, companies are beginning to ask: "How can we best exploit the Internet for our business?" Initially, companies were using the Internet to promote their company's image, products, and services by providing World Wide Web access to corporate Web sites. Today, however, the Internet potential is limitless, and the focus has shifted to e-business, using the global reach of the Internet for easy access to key business applications and data that reside in traditional I/T systems. Companies can now securely and cost-effectively extend the reach of their applications and data across the world through the implementation of secure virtual private network (VPN) solutions.

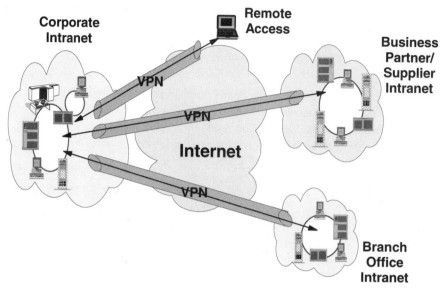

Figure 1. *Virtual Private Networks*

A virtual private network (VPN) is an extension of an enterprise's private intranet across a public network such as the Internet, creating a secure private connection, essentially through a private *tunnel*. VPNs securely convey information across the Internet connecting remote users, branch offices, and business partners into an extended corporate network, as shown in Figure 1. Internet Service Providers (ISPs) offer cost-effective access to the Internet (via direct lines or local telephone numbers), enabling companies to eliminate their current, expensive leased lines, long-distance calls, and toll-free telephone numbers.

A 1997 VPN Research Report, by Infonetics Research, Inc., estimates savings from 20% to 47% of wide area network (WAN) costs by replacing leased lines to remote sites with VPNs. And, for remote access VPNs, savings can be 60% to 80% of corporate remote access dial-up costs. Additionally, Internet access is available worldwide where other connectivity alternatives may not be available.

The technology to implement these virtual private networks, however, is just becoming standardized. Some networking vendors today are offering non-standards-based VPN solutions that make it difficult for a company to incorporate all its employees and/or business partners/suppliers into an extended corporate network. However, VPN solutions based on Internet Engineering Task Force (IETF) standards will provide support for the full range of VPN scenarios with more interoperability and expansion capabilities.

The key to maximizing the value of a VPN is the ability for companies to evolve their VPNs as their business needs change and to easily upgrade to future TCP/IP technology. Vendors who support a broad range of hardware and software VPN products provide the flexibility to meet these requirements. VPN solutions today run mainly in the IPv4 environment, but it is important that they have the capability of being upgraded to IPv6 to remain interoperable with your business partner's and/or supplier's VPN solutions. Perhaps equally critical is the ability to work with a vendor who understands the issues of deploying a VPN. The implementation of a successful VPN involves more than technology. The vendor's networking experience plays heavily into this equation.

1.2 Security Considerations for VPNs

The use of VPNs raises several security concerns beyond those that were present in traditional corporate networks. A typical end-to-end data path might contain:

- Several machines not under control of the corporation (for example, the ISP access box in a dial-in segment and the routers within the Internet).
- A security gateway (firewall or router) that is located at the boundary between an internal segment and an external segment.
- An internal segment (intranet) that contains hosts and routers. Some could be malicious, and some will carry a mix of intra-company and inter-company traffic.
- An external segment (Internet) that carries traffic not only from your company's network but also from other sources.

In this heterogeneous environment, there are many opportunities to eavesdrop, to change a datagram's contents, to mount denial-of-service attacks, or to alter a datagram's destination address, as outlined in the following sections. The IBM solutions provide the tools to counter these threats.

Let us have a look at a typical end-to-end path next so that we will be able to understand the security considerations raised with common scenarios.

1.2.1 A Typical End-to-End Path

To understand the issues with VPN end-to-end security, we look at the elements along an end-to-end path. While not all the elements may appear in a given path, some of them will appear in every VPN configuration. End-to-end traffic will usually flow over a mix of three basic segments: a dial-in segment, an external segment (Internet), and an internal segment (intranet).

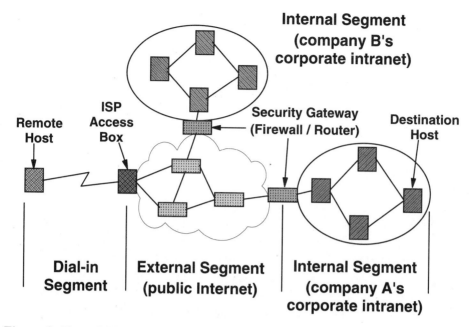

Figure 2. Typical Elements in an End-to-End Path

As shown in Figure 2, a path might include a first-hop dial-in connection to an Internet Service Provider (ISP), who in turn uses the backbone public Internet to carry the user's traffic back to a gateway at the perimeter of the corporate network. Then, the traffic eventually flows within an intranet to its ultimate destination. As we also see in Figure 2, inter-company communication can create a path that includes two separate intranets (for example, company A's and company B's).

For discussion purposes in this redbook, we refer to these elements as outlined below:

- **Dial-in Segment:** In today's environment, remote access has become a necessity. Both work-at-home and on-the-road employees want convenient and secure dial-in access to their company's networks; and sometimes they even need to communicate with hosts located inside another company's network. We refer to both work-at-home and on-the-road users as *remote users*. This segment extends from a remote user's machine to an access box provided by the ISP. The protocols and procedures used on this link are specified by the Internet Service Provider. Today, most ISPs support the Point-to-Point Protocol (PPP) suite of protocols on this segment.

- **External Network (Internet):** The Internet is not owned or operated by any single entity, but is a collection of distinct routing domains, each operated by a different authority. The unifying factor is the standardized IP communications protocols defined by the Internet Engineering Task Force (IETF). The Internet Protocol (IP) suite of protocols will route data traffic at the network layer over a path that may span several ISPs' routing domains. Since IP is a connectionless technology, each user datagram could potentially follow a different path. And in fact, traffic from several different companies could all flow simultaneously through a given backbone router in the Internet. For example, a datagram that originated in company A's intranet and a datagram that originated in company B's intranet could both flow through a common router located somewhere in the Internet. A company's traffic on the Internet can no longer be considered to be isolated from the outside world, as it would have been on a dedicated private network, since flows from different VPNs will be intermixed on the Internet backbone.

- **Internal Network (intranet):** This segment appears at an endpoint of the communications path. It is under the control of the corporation, who typically operates and manages it. Traditionally, almost all traffic flowing within a corporate network was generated by the corporation's employees; very little traffic entered or exited the corporate network; and the protocols in the intranet were proprietary.

  Today, IP is becoming a popular protocol for use within corporate intranets, and data traffic enters and exits the corporate intranet regularly (consider Web browsers, ftp, or telnet applications). In today's world of e-business, there are emerging requirements for external suppliers and business partners to have access to data stored on another company's internal servers. Since traffic flowing within an intranet at any given time may have been generated by several different companies, today it may no longer be possible to categorize a given intranet as *trusted* or *untrusted*. A company may consider its own intranets to be trusted, but at the same time its business partners may consider it to be untrusted. In this environment, a VPN designer may need to provide network security functions both on the intranet segments and on the Internet segment.

As shown in Figure 2 on page 4, there are four classes of machines that occur along the path:

- Remote hosts (dial-up)
- Fixed hosts (sources and destinations, or clients and servers)
- ISP access box
- Security gateways (firewalls and/or routers)

Protocols in these machines are used to provide address assignment, tunneling, and IP security. Viable security solutions can be constructed by deploying IP security in some combination of remote hosts, firewalls, routers, and fixed hosts. But since each company should be responsible for its own security, there is no requirement for the ISP boxes or the routers in the Internet backbone to support IP security.

1.2.2 Exposures in a Dial-In Segment

The dial-in segment in Figure 2 on page 4 delivers a user's data traffic directly to an Internet Service Provider (ISP). If the data is in cleartext (that is, not encrypted), then it is very easy for the ISP to examine sensitive user data, or for an attacker to eavesdrop on the data as it travels over the dial-in link.

Link-layer encryption between the remote host and the ISP can protect against passive eavesdropping, but it does not protect against a malicious ISP. Since the ISP can decrypt the user's data stream, sensitive data is still available to the ISP in cleartext format.

1.2.3 Exposures in the Internet

In some remote-access scenarios, an ISP builds a tunnel to extend the reach of the PPP connection so that its endpoints will be the access box and the security gateway. If the tunneling protocol does not incorporate robust security features, a malicious ISP could easily build a tunnel that terminates somewhere other than at the correct security gateway (see Figure 3). Thus, user's data could be delivered via a false tunnel to a malicious impostor gateway where it could be examined or even altered.

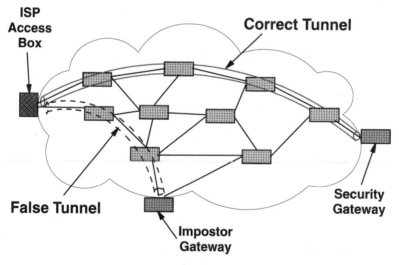

Figure 3. Exposures in the External (Internet) Segment

There are also dangers as the datagram travels within the tunnel. As illustrated in Figure 3, user datagrams pass through routers in the Internet as they travel along a path toward the tunnel endpoint. If the datagrams are in cleartext, any of these routers could easily examine or modify the datagram, and passive attackers could eavesdrop on any of the links along the path.

Link-by-link encryption at each hop in the Internet backbone can thwart eavesdroppers, but does not protect the user's data from a malicious router, since each router along the path would be capable of decrypting the user's data stream. Nor does link-by-link encryption protect against false tunnels, since the false tunnel endpoint would have access to cleartext data.

Even popular tunneling protocols such as Layer 2 Tunneling Protocol (L2TP) do not provide robust security. Therefore the IETF has recommended that the tunnel traffic should be protected with the IPSec protocols.

1.2.4 Exposures in a Security Gateway

The security gateway (firewall/router) shown in Figure 2 on page 4 also creates security exposures. Its main purpose is to enforce an access control policy (that is, to accept only the desired inbound traffic, to reject undesired inbound traffic, and to prevent internally generated traffic from indiscriminately leaving the corporate network). The firewall or router is under the control of the corporate network, but an internal attacker still has an opportunity to examine any traffic that the gateway decrypts and then forwards into the intranet in cleartext form.

Non-cryptographic authentication provides some protection against unwanted traffic entering or leaving the network. Common techniques are passwords, packet filtering, and network address translation. However, these can be defeated by a variety of well-known attacks, such as address spoofing, and new attacks are being developed regularly. Each time a new packet filter is designed to thwart a known attack, hackers will devise a new attack, which in turn demands that a new filter rule be generated.

Because the cryptography-based authentication techniques require a long time to break, even with powerful computers, it becomes prohibitively expensive, both in time and in computer power, for a hacker to attempt to attack them. Hence, companies can deploy them with the confidence that they will provide robust protection against a hacker's attacks.

Link-by-link encryption does not prevent an intermediate box along the path from monitoring, altering, or rerouting valid traffic, since each intermediate box will have access to the cleartext form of all messages. Even host-to-gateway encryption suffers from the same weakness; the gateway still has access to cleartext.

1.2.5 Exposures in an Intranet

Although there is a popular belief that most security threats will occur in the public Internet, there have been studies showing that many of the attacks actually arise internally. Unless every host, gateway, and router within the intranet of Figure 2 on page 4 can be fully trusted, it is possible for a malicious employee to modify an internal box, making it possible to monitor, alter, or reroute datagrams that flow within the corporate network. When data from several different networks flows within the intranet (for example, in the case where the VPN interconnects a manufacturer's intranet with the intranets of several suppliers) threats within the intranet need to be guarded against. Even if company A trusts that its own intranet is secure, the external supplier or business partner whose traffic must flow through company A's intranet may not trust it; after all, the partner's data is at risk if company A's intranet is in fact compromised in any fashion.

1.2.6 Conclusions

There are security exposures everywhere along an end-to-end path: on the dial-up link, in an ISP's access box, in the Internet, in the firewall or router, and even in the corporate intranet.

Previously, security solutions were developed to address just a subset of the exposures discussed in this section, but there was no framework that could protect against all these exposures using a single approach.

IP Security Architecture (IPSec) is the first definition of a comprehensive, consistent solution. It can provide end-to-end protection as well as segment-by-segment protection. Based on the work of the Internet Engineering Task Force (IETF) IBM chose to use IPSec for its IBM eNetwork VPN solutions.

The next section gives an overview of some VPN implementations available in the market today. We describe the IPSec components in more detail in Chapter 3, "Description of IPSec" on page 47.

1.3 VPN Solutions in the Marketplace

Vendors' VPN offerings can be categorized in a number of ways. In our opinion the most important differentiator is the protocol layer on which the VPN is realized. In this context, there are the following different approaches to VPN implementation:

- Network layer-based (IPSec-based)

- Data link layer-based (layer 2-based)

There are other methods that operate on upper layers and complement a VPN solution, such as SOCKS, Secure Sockets Layer (SSL), or Secure Multipurpose Internet Mail Extension (S-MIME). Some vendors' solutions use only the upper layer protocols to construct a VPN, usually a combination of SOCKS V5 and SSL. In Figure 4 on page 9 the TCP/IP layered protocol stack is shown, with the VPN related protocols associated to each layer. A description of these can be found in 1.3.3, "Non-IPSec Network Layer-Based Components of a VPN Solution" on page 15.

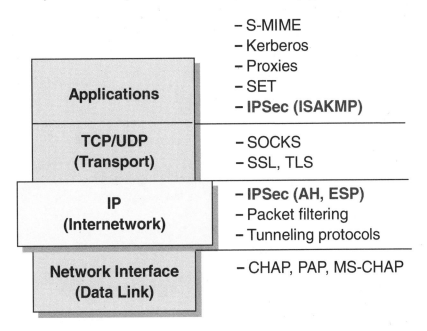

Figure 4. The TCP/IP Protocol Stack and the VPN-Related Protocols

1.3.1 IPSec-Based VPN Solutions

Within the layered communications protocol stack model, the network layer (IP in the case of the TCP/IP stack) is the lowest layer that can provide end-to-end security. Network-layer security protocols provide blanket protection for all upper-layer application data carried in the payload of an IP datagram, without requiring a user to modify the applications.

The solutions are based on the IP Security Architecture (IPSec) open framework, defined by the IPSec Working Group of the IETF. IPSec is called a framework because it provides a stable, long lasting base for providing network layer security. It can accommodate today's cryptographic algorithms, and can also accommodate newer, more powerful algorithms as they become available. IPv6 implementations are required to support IPSec, and IPv4 implementations are strongly recommended to do so. In addition to providing the base security functions for the Internet, IPSec furnishes flexible building blocks from which robust, secure virtual private networks can be constructed.

The IPSec Working Group has concentrated on defining protocols to address several major areas:

- *Data origin authentication* verifies that each datagram was originated by the claimed sender.

- *Data integrity* verifies that the contents of the datagram were not changed in transit, either deliberately or due to random errors.

- *Data confidentiality* conceals the cleartext of a message, typically by using encryption.

- *Replay protection* assures that an attacker can not intercept a datagram and play it back at some later time without being detected.

- *Automated management of cryptographic keys and security associations* assures that a company's VPN policy can be conveniently and accurately implemented throughout the extended network with little or no manual configuration. These functions make it possible for a VPN's size to be scaled to whatever size a business requires.

Note: The above mentioned areas (among others) are the subject of the discipline of cryptography. For a short introduction to cryptography see Chapter 2, "A Short Introduction to Cryptography" on page 27.

The principal IPSec protocols are:

- IP Authentication Header (AH) provides data origin authentication, data integrity, and replay protection.
- IP Encapsulating Security Payload (ESP) provides data confidentiality, data origin authentication, data integrity, and replay protection.
- Internet Security Association and Key Management Protocol (ISAKMP) provides a method for automatically setting up security associations and managing their cryptographic keys.

1.3.1.1 Authentication Header (AH)

The IP Authentication Header provides connectionless (that is, per-packet) integrity and data origin authentication for IP datagrams, and also offers protection against replay. Data integrity is assured by the checksum generated by a message authentication code (for example, MD5); data origin authentication is assured by including a secret shared key in the data to be authenticated; and replay protection is provided by use of a sequence number field within the AH header. In the IPSec vocabulary, these three distinct functions are lumped together and simply referred to by the name *authentication*.

1.3.1.2 Encapsulating Security Payload (ESP)

The IP Encapsulating Security Payload provides data confidentiality (encryption), connectionless (that is per-packet) integrity, data origin authentication, and protection against replay. ESP always provides data confidentiality, and can also optionally provide data origin authentication, data integrity checking, and replay protection. Comparing ESP to AH, one sees that only ESP provides encryption, while either can provide authentication, integrity checking, and replay protection.

When ESP is used to provide authentication functions, it uses the same algorithms used by the AH protocol. However, the coverage is different.

1.3.1.3 Combining the Protocols

Either ESP or AH may be applied alone, in combination with the other, or even nested within another instance of itself. With these combinations, authentication and/or encryption can be provided between a pair of communicating hosts, between a pair of communicating firewalls, or between a host and a firewall.

1.3.1.4 ISAKMP/Oakley

A security association (SA) contains all the relevant information that communicating systems need in order to execute the IPSec protocols, such as AH or ESP. For example, a security association will identify the cryptographic algorithm to be used, the keying information, the identities of the participating parties, etc. ISAKMP defines a standardized framework to support negotiation of security associations (SA), initial generation of all cryptographic keys, and subsequent refresh of these keys. Oakley is the mandatory key management protocol that is required to be used within the ISAKMP framework. ISAKMP supports automated negotiation of security associations, and automated generation and refresh of cryptographic keys. The ability to perform these functions with little or no manual configuration of machines will be a critical element as a VPN grows in size.

Secure exchange of keys is the most critical factor in establishing a secure communications environment—no matter how strong your authentication and encryption are, they are worthless if your key is compromised. Since the ISAKMP procedures deal with initializing the keys, they must be capable of running over links *where no security can be assumed to exist*. That is, they are used to *bootstrap* the

IPSec protocols. Hence, the ISAKMP protocols use the most complex and processor-intensive operations in the IPSec protocol suite.

ISAKMP requires that all information exchanges must be both encrypted and authenticated. No one can eavesdrop on the keying material, and the keying material will be exchanged only among authenticated parties.

1.3.1.5 The Vendors

An IPSec-based VPN can be built in many different ways according to the user's needs. In the general case, a combination of clients, servers, firewalls and routers are using IPSec technology. These components might come from different vendors, thus interoperability is a major requirement.

Without attempting to be complete, here is an enumeration of the active players in this field: Ascend, Bay Networks, Checkpoint, Cisco, Hewlett Packard, IBM, Intel, Sun, 3Com. These companies offer one or more of the following: IPSec-enabled stacks for different operating system platforms, IPSec-enabled firewall software and IPSec-enabled routers. Microsoft has announced IPSec support for Version 5 of their Windows NT operating system.

In the view of IBM, since the needs of companies differ significantly, any VPN implementation is likely to be custom-made, and should therefore include service and support. In order to meet these customer requirements, IBM has developed the eNetwork Virtual Private Network, an industrial strength VPN solution that incorporates a wide range of client, server, firewall and router offerings, with installation and maintenance for ease of use.

Please refer to Chapter 3, "Description of IPSec" on page 47 for a technical description of the IPSec framework and to Appendix A, "IBM eNetwork VPN Solutions" on page 119 for details on the IBM eNetwork VPN offerings.

1.3.2 Layer 2-Based VPN Solutions

A remote access dial-up solution for mobile users is a very simple form of a virtual private network, typically used to support dial-in access to a corporate network whose users are all company employees. To eliminate the long-distance charges that would occur if a remote user were to dial-in directly to a gateway on the home network, the IETF developed a tunneling protocol, Layer 2 Tunnel Protocol (L2TP). This protocol extends the span of a PPP connection: instead of beginning at the remote host and ending at a local ISP's point of presence (PoP), the *virtual PPP* link now extends from the remote host all the way back to the corporate gateway. In effect, the remote host appears to be on the same subnet as the corporate gateway.

Since the host and the gateway share the same PPP connection, they can take advantage of PPP's ability to transport protocols other than just IP. For example, L2TP tunnels can be used to support remote LAN access as well as remote IP access. Figure 5 on page 13 outlines a basic L2TP configuration:

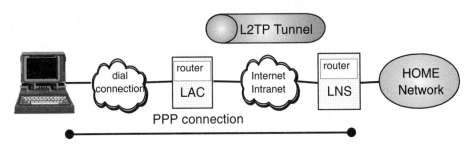

LAC = L2TP access concentrator
LNS = L2TP network server

Figure 5. Layer 2 Tunnel Protocol (L2TP) Scenario

Although L2TP provides cost-effective access, multiprotocol transport, and remote LAN access, it does not provide cryptographically robust security features. For example:

- Authentication is provided only for the identity of tunnel endpoints , but not for each individual packet that flows inside the tunnel. This can expose the tunnel to man-in-the-middle and spoofing attacks.

- Without per-packet integrity, it is possible to mount denial-of-service attacks by generating bogus control messages that can terminate either the L2TP tunnel or the underlying PPP connection.

- L2TP itself provides no facility to encrypt user data traffic. This can lead to embarrassing exposures when data confidentiality is an issue.

- While the payload of the PPP packets can be encrypted, the PPP protocol suite does not provide mechanisms for automatic key generation or for automatic key refresh. This can lead to someone listening in on the wire to finally break that key and gain access to the data being transmitted.

Realizing these shortcomings, the PPP Extensions Working Group of the IETF considered how to remedy these shortfalls. Some members proposed to develop new IPSec-like protocols for use with PPP and L2TP. But since this work would have substantially duplicated the more mature work of the IPSec Working Group, the IETF took the position instead to support the use of the existing IPSec protocols to protect the data that flows through an L2TP tunnel.

L2TP is actually another variation of an IP encapsulation protocol. As shown in Figure 6 on page 14, an L2TP tunnel is created by encapsulating an L2TP frame inside a UDP packet, which in turn is encapsulated inside an IP packet whose source and destination addresses define the tunnel's endpoints. Since the outer encapsulating protocol is IP, clearly IPSec protocols can be applied to this composite IP packet, thus protecting the data that flows within the L2TP tunnel. AH, ESP, and ISAKMP/Oakley protocols can all be applied in a straightforward way.

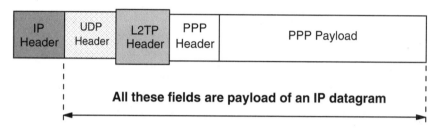

Figure 6. *L2TP Tunnel Encapsulation In IP*

The following reference provides additional information on how to use IPSec in conjunction with L2TP:

```
http://www.ietf.org/internet-drafts/draft-ietf-pppext-l2tp-security-02.txt
```

In summary, layer 2 tunnel protocols are an excellent way of providing cost-effective remote access. And when used in conjunction with IPSec, they are an excellent technique for providing secure remote access. However, without complementary use of IPSec, an L2TP tunnel alone does not furnish adequate security for the solutions that we discuss later in this redbook.

L2TP is a consensus standard that came from the merging of two earlier tunneling protocols: Point-to-Point Tunneling Protocol (PPTP) and Layer 2 Forwarding (L2F; described in RFC 2341). These earlier protocols did not provide as complete a solution as the L2TP protocol; one addresses tunnels created by ISPs and the other addresses tunnels created by remote hosts. L2TP supports both host-created and ISP-created tunnels. As far as vendors are considered, Microsoft incorporates its proprietary PPTP protocol into its Windows NT and Windows 95 operating systems. Cisco offers L2F and L2TP capabilities in its midrange and high-end router product line. The following IBM products will provide L2TP support (besides IPSec) by June 1998:

- IBM Nways Multiprotocol Routing Services Version 3.1, which is the licensed software for the IBM 2210 router family (L2TP support was in fact already available with Version 2.2)

- IBM Nways Multiprotocol Access Services Version 3.1, which is the licensed software for the IBM 2216 router family

Note: L2TP will not available on the 1x4 models of the IBM 2210 family.

Please see the IBM redbook *A Comprehensive Guide to Virtual Private Networks, Volume II: IBM Nways Router Solutions*, SG24-5234, to be published later this year, for more information on how to implement L2TP scenarios with the IBM 2210 and 2216 routers.

1.3.3 Non-IPSec Network Layer-Based Components of a VPN Solution

The IPSec framework provides security for the network layer of the protocol stack. That is, it provides security functions between pairs of machines that have verifiable network layer identities (such as the IP address, fully qualified domain names, and so on). However, IPSec does not work in isolation. Other protocols and functions can be employed to complement IPSec's security functions, for example by providing finer granularity over the material to be protected. For example, efficient Certificate Management functions can make IPSec easier to deploy, and upper layer security functions, such as Secure Sockets Layer (SSL) can provide application level security in addition to IPSec's network layer security. Or a centralized VPN policy directory that can be accessed with a protocol such as Lightweight Directory Access Protocol (LDAP) can make it easier to configure systems correctly without tedious manual operations.

The following sections explain several services and protocols as they relate to IPSec. Designers of VPNs should keep in mind that these techniques are complementary to IPSec, and in many cases can be used in conjunction with IPSec to provide very fine-grained protection of applications in cases where it is needed.

We already took a look at IPSec, which is located at the network layer. Let us see what other functionality is offered at this layer.

1.3.3.1 Network Address Translation

Sometimes globally unique IP addresses are a scarce resource. For example, in Europe, it is especially hard to obtain a globally unique IPv4 address. Other times, a company simply wishes to keep secret the IP addresses of the machines in its intranet (an unlisted address, similar in concept to an unlisted phone number). Both of these situations can be addressed with a function called Network Address Translation (NAT).

Network Address Translation (NAT) is usually implemented in a machine that resides at the boundary of a company's intranet, at the point where there is a link to the public Internet. In most cases this machine will be a firewall or router. NAT sets up and maintains a mapping between internal IP addresses and external public (globally unique) IP addresses. Because the internal addresses are not advertised outside of the intranet, NAT can be used when they are private (globally ambiguous) addresses, or when they are public (globally unique) addresses that a company wishes to keep secret.

The weakness of NAT in context to VPNs is that by definition the NAT-enabled machine will change some or all of the address information in an IP packet. When end-to-end IPSec authentication is used, a packet whose address has been changed will always fail its integrity check under the AH protocol, since any change to any bit in the datagram will invalidate the integrity check value that was generated by the source.

Within the IETF, there is a working group that is looking at the deployment issues surrounding NAT. This group has been advised by the Internet Engineering Steering Group (IESG) that the IETF will not endorse any deployment of NAT that would lead to weaker security that can be obtained when NAT is not used. Since NAT makes it impossible to authenticate a packet using IPSec's AH protocol, NAT should be considered as a temporary measure at best, but should not be pursued as a long term solution to the addressing problem when dealing with secure VPNs.

IPSec protocols offer some solutions to the addressing issues that were previously handled with NAT. We see in later scenarios that there is no need for NAT when all the hosts that comprise a given virtual private network use globally unique (public) IP addresses. Address hiding can be achieved by IPSec's tunnel mode. If a company uses private addresses within its intranet, IPSec's tunnel mode can keep them from ever appearing in cleartext form in the public Internet, which eliminates the need for NAT.

Note: Be careful about NAT issues in conjunction with VPNs. If you are using private IP addresses and have a need to access public resources on the Internet, you are likely to have a need for NAT. If you are going to deploy an IPSec-based VPN, there are scenarios where using NAT would be detrimental to what you are trying to achieve.

1.3.3.2 Packet Filtering

Packet filtering is a technique that is commonly provided in many firewall and router products and in many routers. Packet filtering relies on having access to cleartext; that is, the contents of the IP datagram can not be encrypted or compressed. The machine examines the contents of an IP packet (typically the IP header and the TCP header, and sometimes even the contents of the TCP payload) looking for things such as source addresses, destination addresses, protocol IDs, port numbers, etc. The firewall or router then applies a set of detailed filtering rules to this information to make a decision on whether to accept or reject the packet.

There are various degrees of complexity in filtering. *Stateless* inspection makes a decision on each packet individually, while *stateful* inspection makes a decision for a given packet based on both the packet itself and its history. For example, the history for the TCP protocol could involve monitoring whether or not the TCP handshake messages occur in the correct order within an acceptable time interval.

The advantage of packet filtering is that it provides excellent granularity for making access control decisions. But this is also one of its weaknesses, since the granularity can only be achieved through the specification of elaborate, detailed filtering rules. Rules development tends to be a tedious, error-prone process. And, even if a robust set of rules is in place, they are vulnerable to relatively crude *spoofing attacks*. As new attacks are discovered, firewall administrators end up on a treadmill. Each attack must be countered with very specific new rules, but these new rules don't offer protection against the next new attack.

The major drawback to packet filtering techniques in context to VPNs is that they require access to cleartext, both in packet headers (for stateless inspection) and in the packet payloads (for stateful inspection). When encryption is applied, some or all of the information needed by the packet filters may no longer be available. For example:

- In transport mode, ESP will encrypt the payload of the IP datagram, thus precluding the use of stateful inspection techniques.

- In tunnel mode, ESP will encrypt the entire original datagram, both header and payload, thus precluding stateless or stateful inspection of the original datagram.

IPSec offers a way out of this dilemma. Its AH protocol offers a cryptographically robust and spoof-proof way to enforce access control, and its HMAC algorithms are robust enough that they can not be broken by most hackers. The processor power and the time needed to break them are both prohibitively expensive.

In most IPSec-based VPNs, packet filtering will no longer be the principal method for enforcing access control. IPSec's AH protocol, which is cryptographically robust, will fill that role. Both the number and the complexity of filtering rules will be greatly reduced, and they will be used for fine-tuning only after a packet has already been successfully authenticated by IPSec. And since IPSec's authentication and encryption protocols can be applied simultaneously to a given packet, strong access control can be enforced even when the data itself is encrypted.

If the security gateway (firewall or router) is the endpoint of the tunnel, it still enables you to use packet filtering between itself and the destination host in the secure network, because the packet filters are evaluated before a packet is sent to the IPSec kernel, that is, before applying authentication and/or encryption.

Modern routers also offer packet filtering on a physical port level which allows you to restrict access to secure networks all together, or to redirect traffic, tunneled or otherwise, to a specific port based on the destination address. In that case, access to cleartext is not required but the practical use in a VPN environment may be limited to a subset of possible configurations.

1.3.3.3 Quality-of-Service (QOS)

In a virtual private network, just as in a conventional network, there will be a desire to provide distinct transport characteristics (quality of service) for packets as they travel from source to destination. The IP protocol provides Type of Service (TOS) bits that can be used for this purpose. The details of how to use these bits is a relatively new item of work in the IETF, so no firm standard solutions exist today. However, looking forward to future requirements, the IPSec's AH protocol treats the TOS bits as *mutable*, thus allowing them to be changed as needed while an IPSec protected datagram travels throught the Internet. Thus, IPSec is already positioned to take advantage of the emerging QOS work as soon as it matures.

1.3.4 Non-IPSec Application Layer-Based Components of a VPN Solution

Many firewalls provide application gateways. This technique requires the firewall to be aware of those applications that it will permit to flow across the boundary of a corporate intranet. The user connects to the firewall, which terminates the application. Then, the firewall launches another copy of the same application, running it between itself and the external destination. The firewall then provides synchronization between the internal application (user-to-firewall) and the external application (firewall-to-destination).

1.3.4.1 SOCKS

SOCKS is located at the session layer of the OSI model. The client usually connects to the firewall at port 1080. The firewall then establishes a separate session to the destination host, making the client invisible to the destination host. A drawback is that the client applications need to be *socksified*, which means they have to implement the socks protocol, since it is located at a higher layer than IPSEC the performance of socks is slower than IPSEC. On the other hand this higher layer gives it also more possibilities to control the session.

1.3.4.2 Secure Socket Layer (SSL)

Secure Socket Layer (SSL) is an upper-layer mechanism commonly used by Web browser clients and servers to provide peer authentication and encryption of application data. SSL mandates that the server authenticate itself to the client via a certificate-based technique. Authentication of the client to the server is optional in SSL Version 3, but is not commonly used in practice. SSL involves a handshake phase, where certificates are exchanged, session keys are generated, and encryption algorithms are agreed to. After the handshake phase, user data will be exchanged securely without the need for the application to be explicitly modified, other than to invoke the SSL services before actual data transfer begins.

SSL is an end-to-end protocol, and therefore will be implemented in the machines at the endpoints of a given path (typically the client and the server), but it is not implemented in the intermediate machines along a given path (such as routers or firewalls). Although in theory SSL could be used to protect any TCP/IP application, it is almost exclusively used for HTTP. The client uses any non-privileged port and the server uses port 443.

1.3.4.3 Secure HTTP (S-HTTP)

S-HTTP is a security addition to HTTP. It provides authentication and optionally also encryption. Although it is more flexible than SSL, S-HTTP is rarely used in practice as SSL is easier to administer and has proved functionally adequate for most secure Web applications. Web pages that use S-HTTP have a URL starting with https://. The client uses any non-privileged port and the server uses port 80 (such as HTTP).

1.3.4.4 Secure Mail (S-MIME)

Secure Multipurpose Internet Mail Extension (S-MIME) can be thought of as a very specific SSL-like protocol. S-MIME is an application-level security construct, but its use is limited to protecting e-mail via encryption and digital signatures. It relies on public key technology, and uses X.509 certificates to establish the identities of the communicating parties. S-MIME may be implemented in the communicating end systems; it is not used by intermediate routers or firewalls.

1.3.5 Conclusions

Neither network layer-based nor application layer-based security techniques are the best choice for all situations. There will be trade-offs. Network layer security protects the information created by upper layer protocols, but it requires that IPSec be implemented in the communications stack. With network layer security, there is no need to modify existing upper layer applications. On the other hand, if security features are already imbedded within a given application, then the data for that specific application will be protected while it is in transit, even in the absence of network layer security. Therefore security functions must be imbedded on a per-application basis.

There are still other considerations:

- Network layer security gives "blanket protection", but this may not be as fine-grained as would be desired for a given application. It protects all traffic and is transparent to users and applications.
- Network layer security does not provide protection once the datagram has arrived at its destination host. That is, it is vulnerable to attack within the upper layers of the protocol stack at the destination machine.
- Application layer security can protect the information that has been generated within the upper layers of the stack, but it offers no protection against several common network layer attacks while the datagram is in transit. For example, a datagram in transit would be vulnerable to spoofing attacks against its source or destination address.
- Application layer security is more intelligent (as it knows the application) but also more complex and slower.

Many cases can occur, each of which needs to be examined on its own merit. It may be desirable to employ a mix of both network layer security techniques and application layer techniques to achieve the desired overall level of protection. For example, you could use an upper layer mechanism such as Secure Sockets Layer (SSL) to encrypt upper layer data. SSL could then be supplemented with IPSec's AH protocol at the network layer to provide per-packet data origin authentication and protection against spoofing attacks.

1.4 VPN Customer Scenarios

In this section we look at the three most likely business scenarios well suited to the implementation of a VPN solution.

1. Branch office connection network

2. Business partner/supplier network

3. Remote access network

This section provides a general, overview-type description of those scenarios. Technical issues and configuration details are provided in Chapter 5, "Branch Office Connection Scenario" on page 89, Chapter 6, "Business Partner/Supplier Network Scenario" on page 103, and Chapter 7, "Remote Access Scenario" on page 111, respectively.

1.4.1 Branch Office Connection Network

The branch office scenario securely connects two trusted intranets within your organization. This is a key difference, since your security focus is on both protecting your company's intranet against external intruders and securing your company's data while it flows over the public Internet. This differs from the business partner/supplier network discussed in 1.4.2, "Business Partner/Supplier Network" on page 22, where the focus is on enabling your business partners/suppliers access to data in your corporate intranet.

For example, suppose corporate headquarters wants to minimize the costs incurred from communicating to and among its own branches. Today, the company may use frame relay and/or leased lines, but wants to explore other options for transmitting their internal confidential data that will be less expensive, more secure, and globally accessible. By exploiting the Internet, branch office connection VPNs can easily be established to meet the company's needs.

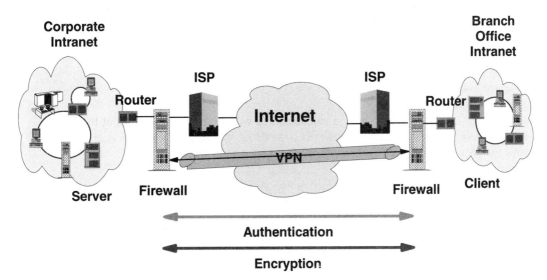

Figure 7. Branch Office Connection Network

As shown in Figure 7, one way to implement this VPN connection between the corporate headquarters and one of its branch offices is for the company to purchase Internet access from an ISP, such as IBM Global Services. IBM eNetwork firewalls, or routers with integrated firewall functionality, or in some cases an IBM server with IPSec capability, would be placed at the boundary of each of the intranets to protect the corporate traffic from Internet hackers. With this scenario, the clients and servers need not support IPSec technology, since the IPSec-enabled firewalls (or routers) would be providing the necessary data packet authentication and encryption. With this approach, any confidential information would be hidden from untrusted Internet users, with the firewall denying access to potential attackers.

With the establishment of branch office connection VPNs, the company's corporate headquarters will be able to communicate securely and cost-effectively to its branches, whether located locally or far away. Through VPN technology, each branch can also extend the reach of its existing intranet to incorporate the other branch intranets, building an extended, enterprise-wide corporate network.

And, as in the business partner/supplier network scenario, this company can easily expand this newly created environment to include its business partners, suppliers, and remote users, through the use of open IPSec technology.

1.4.2 Business Partner/Supplier Network

Industry-leading companies will be those that can communicate inexpensively and securely to their business partners, subsidiaries, and vendors. Many companies have chosen to implement frame relay and/or purchase leased lines to achieve this interaction. But this is often expensive, and geographic reach may be limited. VPN technology offers an alternative for companies to build a private and cost-effective extended corporate network with worldwide coverage, exploiting the Internet or other public network.

Suppose you are a major parts supplier to a manufacturer. Since it is critical that you have the specific parts and quantities at the exact time required by the manufacturing firm, you always need to be aware of the manufacturer's inventory status and production schedules. Perhaps you are handling this interaction manually today, and have found it to be time consuming, expensive and maybe even inaccurate. You'd like to find an easier, faster, and more effective way of communicating. However, given the confidentiality and time-sensitive nature of this information, the manufacturer does not want to publish this data on their corporate Web page or distribute this information monthly via an external report.

To solve these problems, the parts supplier and manufacturer can implement a VPN, as shown in Figure 8 on page 23. A VPN can be built between a client workstation, in the parts supplier's intranet, directly to the server residing in the manufacturer's intranet. The clients can authenticate themselves either to the firewall or router protecting the manufacturer's intranet, directly to the manufacturer's server (validating that they are who they say they are), or to both, depending on your security policy. Then a tunnel could be established, encrypting all data packets from the client, through the Internet, to the required server.

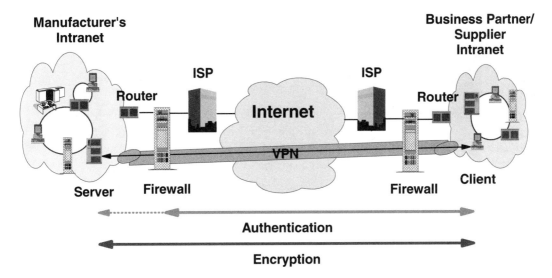

Figure 8. *Business Partner/Supplier Network*

With the establishment of this VPN, the parts supplier can have global, online access to the manufacturer's inventory plans and production schedule at all times during the day or night, minimizing manual errors and eliminating the need for additional resources for this communication. In addition, the manufacturer can be assured that the data is securely and readily available to only the intended parts supplier(s).

One way to implement this scenario is for the companies to purchase Internet access from an Internet service provider (ISP), such as IBM Global Services. Then, given the lack of security of the Internet, either an IBM eNetwork firewall or IPSec-enabled router, or an IBM server with IPSec capability can be deployed as required to protect the intranets from intruders. If end-to-end protection is desired, then both the client and server machines need to be IPSec-enabled as well.

Through the implementation of this VPN technology, the manufacturer would easily be able to extend the reach of their existing corporate intranet to include one or more parts suppliers (essentially building an extended corporate network) while enjoying the cost-effective benefits of using the Internet as their backbone. And, with the flexibility of open IPSec technology, the ability for this manufacturer to incorporate more external suppliers is limitless.

Yet, inherent in network expansion are concerns of manageability. Tools should be implemented to ensure your network remains easy to maintain. Management functions to be included in future eNetwork VPN solutions are:

- Policy management
- Automated ISAKMP/Oakley key management capabilities
- Certificate management
- Secure domain name server (DNS)
- Lightweight Directory Access Protocol (LDAP) support

When implementing a VPN, a set of security configuration criteria must be established. Decisions such as which security algorithms are to be used by each IPSec-enabled box and when the keys are to be refreshed are all aspects of policy management. And, with respect to key technology, almost all of today's currently popular security protocols begin by using public key cryptography. Each user is assigned a unique public key. Certificates, in the form of digital signatures, validate the authenticity of your identity and your encryption key. These certificates can be stored in a public key database, such as a secure DNS, that can be accessible via a simple protocol, such as LDAP.

An automated IP address management system is especially important for VPNs in order to assign and manage your network's IP addresses. IBM is working with an IP address management company to offer highly centralized control of all network devices in your entire extended intranet. Also, along the lines of managing your IP addresses, network address translation (NAT), available today in the eNetwork Firewall for AIX, allows you to use a globally unique (public) address on the Internet, while enabling you to use private IP addresses within your intranet.

IBM will be incorporating all of these VPN management tools into its eNetwork VPN solutions, which can easily be implemented to meet the needs of your existing and future networking environment. The future of VPN is discussed in Chapter 4, "The Internet Key Exchange (IKE) Protocol" on page 71.

1.4.3 Remote Access Network

A remote user, whether at home or on the road, wants to be able to communicate securely and cost-effectively back to his/her corporate intranet. Although many still use expensive long-distance and toll-free telephone numbers, this cost can be greatly minimized by exploiting the Internet. For example, you are at home or on the road, but need a confidential file on a server within your intranet. By obtaining Internet access in the form of a dial-in connection to an ISP such as IBM Global Services, you can communicate with the server in your intranet and access the required file.

One way to implement this scenario is to use an eNetwork VPN IPSec-enabled remote client and firewall, as shown in Figure 9 on page 25. The client accesses the Internet via dial-up to an ISP, and then establishes an authenticated and encrypted tunnel between itself and the firewall at the intranet boundary.

By applying IPSec authentication between the remote client and the firewall, you can protect your intranet from unwanted and possibly malicious IP packets. And by encrypting traffic that flows between the remote host and the firewall, you can prevent outsiders from eavesdropping on your information.

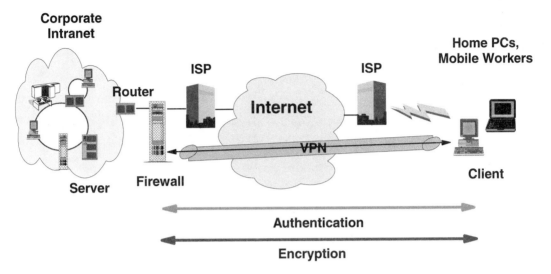

Figure 9. Remote Access Network

The three scenarios discussed in this section are the basis for the IPSec implementation and configuration examples described in this redbook. But before we come to the practical part, we would like to discuss the theory behind cryptography and IPSec in more detail.

Chapter 2. A Short Introduction to Cryptography

The purpose of this chapter is to introduce the terminology and give a brief overview of the major cryptographic concepts that relate to IPSec as a foundation of the virtual private networks. The pivot of any VPN technology is its cryptographic feature set. One should not plan and implement VPNs without knowing what level of security can be achieved with a given technology incorporated in a certain product. After all, you do not want to see your sensitive information at stake when crossing insecure channels.

The information presented here only scratches the surface. Some issues are left open or not mentioned at all. The more interested reader should consult the reference works listed in Appendix D, "Related Publications" on page 157.

2.1 Terminology

Let's start with defining some very basic concepts.

Cryptography

Put simply, cryptography is the science of keeping your data and communications secure. To achieve this goal, techniques such as *encryption, decryption* and *authentication* are used. With the recent advances in this field, the frontiers of cryptography have become blurred. Every procedure consisting of transforming data based on methods that are difficult to reverse can be considered cryptography. The key factor to strong cryptography is the difficulty of reverse engineering. You would be amazed to know that breaking simple methods such as password-scrambled word processor documents or compressed archives is a matter of minutes for a hacker using an ordinary PC. *Strong* cryptography means that the computational effort needed to retrieve your cleartext messages without knowing the proper procedure makes the retrieval infeasible. In this context, infeasible means something like this: if all the computers in the world were assigned to the problem, they would have to work tens of thousands of years until the solution was found. The process of retrieval is called *cryptanalysis*. An attempted cryptanalysis is an *attack*.

Encryption and Decryption - Cryptographic Algorithms

Encryption is the transformation of a cleartext message into an unreadable form in order to hide its meaning. The opposite transformation, which retrieves the original cleartext, is the decryption. The mathematical function used for encryption and decryption is the *cryptographic algorithm* or *cipher*.

The security of a cipher might be based entirely on keeping how it works secret, in which case it is a *restricted* cipher. There are many drawbacks to restricted ciphers. It is very difficult to keep in secret an algorithm used by many people. If it is incorporated in a commercial product, then it is only a matter of time and money to get it reverse engineered. For these reasons, the currently used algorithms are *keyed*, that is, the encryption and decryption makes use of a parameter, the *key*. The key can be chosen from a set of possible values, called the *keyspace*. The keyspace usually is huge, the bigger the better. The security of these algorithms rely entirely on the key, not on their internal secrets. In fact the algorithms themselves are public and are extensively analyzed for possible weaknesses.

Note: As a general rule, be conservative. Do not trust brand new, unknown or unpublished algorithms. The principle of the keyed ciphers is shown in Figure 10.

Figure 10. Keyed Encryption and Decryption

Note: It is common in the cryptographic literature to denote the first participant in a protocol as Alice and the second one as Bob. They are the "crypto couple".

Authentication, Integrity, and Non-Repudiation

Encryption provides confidentiality to your messages. When communicating over an untrusted medium, such as the Internet, besides confidentiality, you need more:

- *Authentication* - A method for verifying that the sender of a message is really he or she claims to be. Any intruder masquerading as someone else is detected by authentication.

- *Integrity checking* - A method for verifying that a message has not been altered along the communication path. Any tampered message sent by an intruder is detected by integrity check. As a side effect, communication errors are also detected.

- *Non-repudiation* - The possibility to prove that the sender has really sent the message. When algorithms providing non-repudiation are used, the sender is not able to later deny the fact that he or she sent the message in question.

2.2 Symmetric or Secret-Key Algorithms

The symmetric algorithms are keyed algorithms where the decryption key is the same as the encryption key. These are the conventional cryptographic algorithms where the sender and the receiver must agree on the key *before* any secured communication can take place between them. Figure 10 on page 28 illustrates a symmetric algorithm. There are two types of symmetric algorithms: *block algorithms*, which operate on the cleartext in blocks of bits, and *stream algorithms*, which operate on a single bit (or byte) of cleartext at a time.

Block ciphers are used in several *modes*. *Electronic Codebook Mode (ECB)* is the simplest; each block of cleartext is encrypted independently. Given a block length of 64 bits, there are 2^{64} possible input cleartext blocks, each of them corresponding to exactly one out of 2^{64} possible ciphertext blocks. An intruder might construct a codebook with known cleartext-ciphertext pairs and mount an attack. Because of this vulnerability, often the *Cipher Block Chaining (CBC)* mode is used, where the result of the encryption of the previous block is used in the encryption of the current block, thus each ciphertext block is dependent not just on the corresponding plaintext block, but on all previous plaintext blocks.

The algorithms often make use of *initialization vectors (IVs)*. These are variables independent of the keys and are good for setting up the initial state of the algorithms.

A well-known block algorithm is DES, a worldwide standard cipher developed by IBM. DES is an acronym for Data Encryption Standard. DES operates on 64-bit blocks and has a key length of 56 bits, often expressed as a 64-bit number, with every eighth bit serving as parity bit. From this key 16 subkeys are derived, which are used in the 16 rounds of the algorithm.

DES produces ciphertexts of the same length as the cleartext and the decryption algorithm is exactly the same as the encryption, the only difference being the subkey schedule. These properties makes it very suitable for hardware implementations.

Although DES is aging (its origins dates back to the early '70s), after more then 20 years of analysis the algorithm itself is still considered secure. The most practical attack against it is *brute-force*: try the decryption with all possible keys and look for a meaningful result. The problem is the key length. Given enough money and time, a brute-force attack against the 56-bit key might be feasible; that's why recently a new mode of DES, called triple-DES or 3DES has gained popularity. With triple-DES, the original DES algorithm is applied in three rounds, with two or three different keys. This encryption is thought to be unbreakable for a long time, even with the foreseeable technological advances taken into account.

An exportable version of DES is IBM's Commercial Data Masking Facility or CDMF, which uses a 40-bit key.

Another, more recent block algorithm is the *International Data Encryption Algorithm (IDEA)*. This cipher uses 64-bit blocks and 128-bit keys. It was developed in the early '90s and aimed to replace DES. It is cryptographically strong and faster than DES. Despite this, there is no widespread commercial acceptance, mainly because it is relatively new and not fully analyzed. The most significant use of IDEA is in the freeware secure e-mail package Pretty Good Privacy (PGP).

An example of a stream algorithm is A5, which is used to encrypt digital cellular telephony traffic in the GSM standard, widely used in Europe.

The advantage of the symmetric algorithms is their efficiency. They can be easily implemented in hardware. A major disadvantage is the difficulty of key management. A secure way of exchanging the keys must exist, which is often very hard to implement.

2.2.1 Usage of Symmetric Keys with IPSec

These algorithms are used in the ESP protocol of the IPSec framework. Current specifications require only DES in CBC mode, but triple-DES (Internet Draft specification available) and CDMF (as a vendor-specific option with ISAKMP/Oakley) are also used. Specifications also exist for the usage of IDEA and some other encryption algorithms, however support for these is not widespread.

There are two variants of DES in CBC mode that are used with ESP:

- DES-CBC with a 64-bit initialization vector: The ESP protocol header carries the whole initialization vector. This variant is marked as DES_CBC_8 in the IBM products.

- DES-CBC with a 32-bit initialization vector: The ESP protocol header carries only a 32-bit value as IV, from which the full 64-bit IV is generated by concatenation of the original 32-bit IV and its complement. You can find this variant as DES_CBC_4 in the IBM products.

There is no significant difference in the security level of the variants. DES_CBC_8 has a slightly greater overhead. Most implementations, for example the IBM Firewall, use sequential IVs.

2.3 Asymmetric or Public-Key Algorithms

These algorithms address the major drawback of the symmetric ones, the requirement of the secure key-exchange channel. The idea is that two different keys should be used: a public key, which as the name implies, is known to everyone, and a private key, which is to be kept in tight security by the owner. The private key cannot be determined from the public key. A cleartext encrypted with the public key can only be decrypted with the corresponding private key, and vice versa. A cleartext encrypted with the private key can only be decrypted with the corresponding public key. Thus, if someone sends a message encrypted with the recipient's public key, it can be read by the intended recipient only. The process is shown in Figure 11, where Alice sends an encrypted message to Bob.

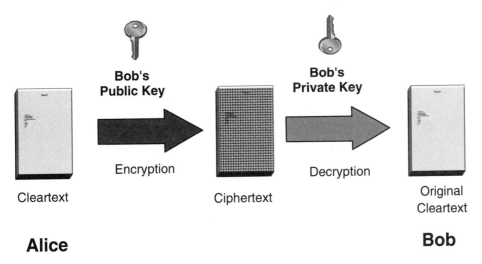

Figure 11. Encryption Using the Recipient's Public Key

As the public key is available to anyone, privacy is assured without the need for a secure key-exchange channel. Parties who wish to communicate retrieve each other's public key.

2.3.1 Authentication and Non-Repudiation

An interesting property of the public-key algorithms is that they can provide authentication. Use the private key for encryption. Since anyone has access to the corresponding public key and can decrypt the message, this provides no privacy. However, it authenticates the message. If one can successfully decrypt it with the claimed sender's public key, then the message has been encrypted with the corresponding private key, which is known by the real sender only. Thus, the sender's identity is verified. The encryption with the private key is used in *digital signatures*. In Figure 12 the principle is shown. Alice encrypts her message with her private key ("signs" it), in order to enable Bob to verify the authenticity of the message.

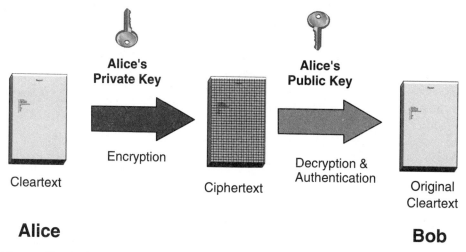

Figure 12. Authentication by Encrypting with a Private Key

Going a step forward, encrypting with the private key gives non-repudiation too. The mere existence of such an encrypted message testifies that the originator has really sent it, because only he or she could have used the private key to generate the message. Additionally, if a timestamp is included, then the exact date and time can also be proven. There are protocols involving trusted third parties that prevent the sender from using phony timestamps.

Note: Inspired by the "stamping" idea, the IPSec architecture makes use of sequence numbers (instead of timestamps), to achieve replay protection.

2.3.2 Examples of Public-Key Algorithms

Algorithms based on public keys can be used for a variety of purposes. Two common applications are:

1. Encryption (see 2.3.3.1, "RSA Public Key Algorithm" on page 34)
2. Generation of shared keys for use with symmetric key algorithms (see 2.3.3.2, "Diffie-Hellman Key Exchange" on page 35)

The most popular public-key algorithm is the de-facto standard *RSA*, named after the three inventors: Ron Rivest, Adi Shamir and Leonard Adleman. The security of RSA relies on the difficult problem of factoring large numbers. The public and private keys are functions of two very large (200 digits or even more) prime numbers. Given the public key and the ciphertext, an attack would be successful if it could factor the product of the two primes. RSA has resisted many years of extensive attacks. As computing power grows, keeping RSA secure is a matter of increasing the key length. (As opposed to DES, where the key length is fixed.)

Another public-key algorithm, actually the very first ever invented, is *Diffie-Hellman*. This is a key-exchange algorithm; that is, it is used for securely establishing a shared secret over an insecure channel. The communicating parties exchange public information from which they derive a key. An eavesdropper cannot reconstruct the key from the information that went through the insecure channel. (More precisely, the reconstruction is computationally infeasible.) The security of Diffie-Hellman relies on the difficulty of calculating discrete logarithms in finite fields. After the shared secret has been established, it can then be used to derive keys for use with symmetric key algorithms such as DES.

Diffie-Hellman makes possible the secure derivation of a shared secret key, but it does not authenticate the parties. For authentication another public-key algorithm must be used, such as RSA.

Unfortunately, public-key algorithms while providing for easier key management, privacy, authentication and non-repudiation also have some disadvantages. The most important one is that they are slow and difficult to implement in hardware. For example, RSA is 100 to 10000 times slower than DES, depending on implementation. Because of this, public-key algorithms generally are not used for bulk encryption. Their most important use is key exchange and authentication. Another notable disadvantage is that they are susceptible to certain cryptanalytic attacks to which symmetric algorithms are resistant.

Therefore, a good cryptographic system (*cryptosystem*) makes use of both worlds. It uses public-key algorithms in the session establishment phase for authentication and key exchange, then a symmetric one for encrypting the consequent messages.

2.3.3 Usage of Asymmetric Keys with IPSec

IPSec uses asymmetric algorithms for secure key generation and authentication. These operations are typical in the ISAKMP/Oakley framework.

For the interested reader, below we give more detailed information of the two most important asymmetric algorithms. Both of them involve modular arithmetics. An arithmetic operation modulo m means that the result of that operation is divided by m and the remainder is taken. For example: 3 * 6 mod 4 = 2, since 3 * 6 = 18 and dividing 18 by 4 gives us 2 as the remainder.

2.3.3.1 RSA Public Key Algorithm

RSA is used in the ISAKMP/Oakley framework as one of the possible authentication methods. The principle of the RSA algorithm is as follows:

1. Take two large primes, p and q.

2. Find their product n = pq; n is called the modulus.

3. Choose a number, e, less than n and relatively prime to (p-1)(q-1) which means that e and (p-1)(q-1) have no common factor other than 1.

4. Find its inverse, d mod (p-1)(q-1) which means that ed = 1 mod (p-1)(q-1).

e and d are called the public and private exponents, respectively. The public key is the pair (n,e); the private key is d. The factors p and q must be kept secret or destroyed.

A simplified example of RSA encryption would be the following:

1. Suppose Alice wants to send a private message, m, to Bob. Alice creates the ciphertext c by exponentiating:

   $c = m^e \bmod n$

   where e and n are Bob's public key.

2. Alice sends c to Bob.

3. To decrypt, Bob exponentiates:

   $m = c^d \bmod n$

and recovers the original message; the relationship between e and d ensures that Bob correctly recovers m. Since only Bob knows d, only Bob can decrypt the ciphertext.

A simplified example of RSA authentication would be the following:

1. Suppose Alice wants to send a signed message, m, to Bob. Alice creates a digital signature s by exponentiating:

   $s = m^d \bmod n$

   where d and n belong to Alice's private key.

2. She sends s and m to Bob.

3. To verify the signature, Bob exponentiates and checks if the result, compares to m:

   $m = s^e \bmod n$

   where e and n belong to Alice's public key.

2.3.3.2 Diffie-Hellman Key Exchange

The Diffie-Hellman key exchange is a crucial component of the ISAKMP/Oakley framework. In the earliest phase of a key negotiation session there is no secure channel in place. The parties derive shared secret keys using the Diffie-Hellman algorithm. These keys will be used in the next steps of the key negotiation protocol.

The outline of the algorithm is the following:

1. The parties (Alice and Bob) share two public values, a modulus m and an integer g; m should be a large prime number.

2. Alice generates a large random number a and computes:

   $X = g^a \bmod m$

3. Bob generates a large random number b and computes:

   $Y = g^b \bmod m$

4. Alice sends X to Bob.

5. Bob computes:

   $K1 = X^b \bmod m$

6. Bob sends Y to Alice.

7. Alice computes:

   $K2 = Y^a \bmod m$

Both K1 and K2 are equal to g^{ab} mod m. This is the shared secret key. Noone is able to generate this value without knowing a or b. The security of the exchange is based on the fact that is extremely difficult to inverse the exponentiation performed by the parties. (In other words, to find out discrete logarithms in finite fields of size m.) Similar to RSA, advances in adversary computing power can be countered by choosing larger initial values, in this case a larger modulus m.

Please see Chapter 4, "The Internet Key Exchange (IKE) Protocol" on page 71 for more details on how ISAKMP/Oakley uses Diffie-Hellman exchanges.

2.4 Hash Functions

Hash functions (also called message digests) are fundamental to cryptography. A hash function is a function that takes variable-length input data and produces fixed length output data (the hash value), which can be regarded as the "fingerprint" of the input. That is, if the hashes of two messages match, then we get a high assurance that the messages are the same.

Cryptographically useful hash functions must be *one-way*, which means that they should be easy to compute, but infeasible to reverse. An everyday example of a one-way function is mashing a potato; it is easy to do, but once mashed, reconstructing the original potato is rather difficult. A good hash function should be *collision-resistant*. It should be hard to find two different inputs that hash to the same value. As any hash function maps an input set to a smaller output set, theoretically it is possible to find collisions. The point is to provide a unique digital "fingerprint" of the message, that identifies it with high confidence, much like a real fingerprint identifying a person.

A hash function that takes a key as a second input parameter and its output depends on both the message and the key is called a *Message Authentication Code (MAC)*, as shown in Figure 13 on page 37.

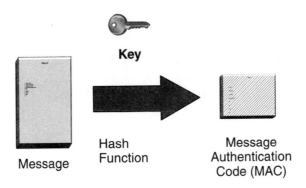

Figure 13. Generating a Message Authentication Code (MAC)

Put simply, if you encrypt a hash, it becomes a MAC. If you add a secret key to a message, then hash the concatenation, the result is a MAC. Both symmetric an asymmetric algorithms can be used to generate MACs.

Hash functions are primarily used in integrity check and authentication techniques. Let's see how integrity and authentication is assured with hash functions:

- The sender calculates the hash of the message and appends it to the message.

- The recipient calculates the hash of the received message and then compares the result with the transmitted hash.

- If the hashes match, the message was not tampered with.

- In case of MACs where the encryption key (symmetric or asymmetric) should have been used by a trusted sender only, a successful MAC decryption indicates that the claimed and actual senders are identical. (Unless, of course, your keys have been compromised.)

See Figure 14 on page 38 for an illustration of the procedure. The Message* and MAC* notations reflect the fact that the message might have been altered while crossing the untrusted channel.

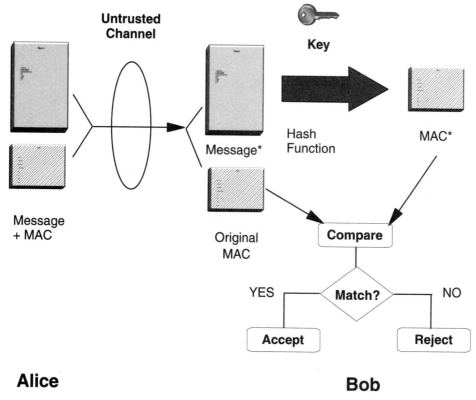

Figure 14. *Checking Integrity and Authenticity with MAC*

One could argue that the same result can be obtained with any kind of encryption, because if an intruder modifies an encrypted message, the decryption will result in nonsense, thus tampering can be detected. The answer is that many times only integrity and/or authentication is needed, maybe with encryption on some of the fields of the message. And encryption is very processor-intensive. (Examples are the personal banking machine networks, where only the PINs are encrypted, however MACs are widely used. Encrypting all the messages in their entirety would not yield noticeable benefits and performance would dramatically decrease.)

The encryption of a hash with the private key is called a *digital signature*. It can be thought of as a special MAC. Using digital signatures instead of encrypting the whole message with the private key leads to considerable performance gains and a remarkable new property. The authentication part can be decoupled from the document itself. This property is used for example in the Secure Electronic Transaction (SET) protocol.

The encryption of a secret key with a public key is called a *digital envelope*. This is a common technique used to distribute secret keys for symmetric algorithms.

Note: In the IPSec vocabulary, the distinct functions of authentication, integrity and replay protection are commonly referred to as authentication. Generally MAC is referred to as authentication data or integrity check value (ICV).

2.4.1 Examples of Hash Functions

The most widely used hash functions are MD5 and Secure Hash Algorithm 1 (SHA-1). MD5 was designed by Ron Rivest (co-inventor of RSA). SHA-1 is largely inspired from MD5 and was designed by the National Institute of Standards and Technology (NIST) and the National Security Agency (NSA) for use with the Digital Signature Standard (DSS). MD5 produces a 128-bit hash, while SHA-1 produces a 160-bit hash. Both functions encode the message length in their output. SHA-1 is regarded as more secure, because of the larger hashes it produces.

Note: Neither MD5 nor SHA-1 takes a key as input parameter, hence in their original implementation they cannot be used for MAC calculation. However, for this purpose it is easy to concatenate a key with the input data and apply the function to the result. In practice, for example in IPSec, often more sophisticated schemes are used.

2.4.2 Usage of Hash Functions with IPSec

The IPSec framework can use both MD5 and SHA-1 for MAC calculation to provide authentication and integrity. There are two ways of using each of the functions, which results in four different possibilities: Keyed MD5, Keyed SHA-1, HMAC-MD5-96 and HMAC-SHA-1-96. Other hash functions can also be accommodated.

2.4.2.1 Keyed MD5 and Keyed SHA-1

Using MD5 and SHA-1 in keyed mode is simple. The shared secret key and the datagram to be protected are both input to the hash algorithm and the output (the hash value) is placed in the Authentication Data field of the AH Header, as it is shown in Figure 15 on page 40.

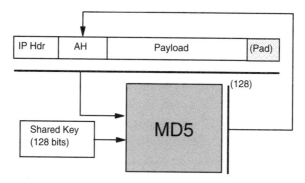

Figure 15. Keyed MD5 Processing

Keyed SHA-1 operates in the same way, the only difference being the larger 160-bit hash value.

2.4.2.2 HMAC-MD5-96 and HMAC-SHA-1-96

A stronger method is the Hashed Message Authentication Code (HMAC), proposed by IBM. HMAC itself is not a hash function, rather a cryptographically strong way to use a specific hash function for MAC calculation.

Here is how HMAC works, considering MD5 as an example. The base function is applied twice in succession. In the first round the input to MD5 is the shared secret key and the datagram. The 128-bit output hash value and the key is input again to the hash function in the second round. The leftmost 96 bits of the resulting hash value are used as the MAC for the datagram. See Figure 16 for an illustration.

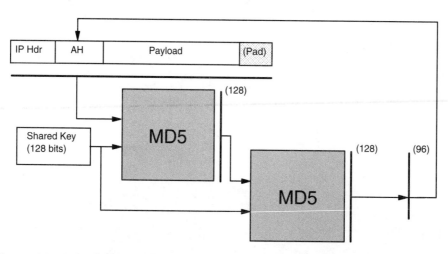

Figure 16. HMAC-MD5-96 Processing

HMAC-SHA-1-96 operates in the same way, except that the intermediary results are 160 bits long.

2.4.2.3 Digital Signature Standard (DSS)

As mentioned previously, a hash value encrypted with the private key is called a *digital signature* and is illustrated in Figure 17.

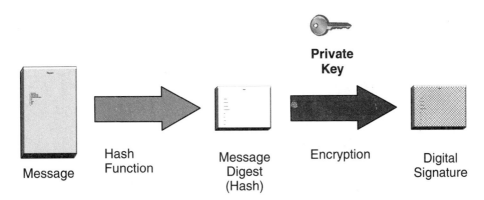

Private Key

| Message | Hash Function | Message Digest (Hash) | Encryption | Digital Signature |

Figure 17. Generating a Digital Signature

One authentication method that can be used with ISAKMP/Oakley is DSS which was selected by NIST and NSA to be the digital authentication standard of the U.S. government. The standard describes the Digital Signature Algorithm (DSA) used to sign and verify signatures of message digests produced with SHA-1.

A brief description of DSA is given below:

1. Choose a large prime number, p, usually between 512 and 1024 bits long.

2. Find a prime factor q of (p-1), 160 bits long.

3. Compute:

   $g = h^{(p-1)/q} \bmod p$

   where h is a number less than (p-1) and the following is true:

   $h^{(p-1)/q} > 1$

4. Choose another number x, less than q, as the sender's private key.

5. Compute:

   $y = g^x \bmod p$

   and use that as the sender's public key. The pair (x,y) is sometimes referred to as the long-term key pair.

6. The sender signs the message as follows:

   a. Generate a random number, k, less than q.
   b. Compute:

   $$r=(g^k \bmod p) \bmod q$$

   $$s=(k^{-1}(\text{SHA1}(m)+xr)) \bmod q$$

   The pair (k,r) is sometimes referred to as the per-session key pair, and the signature is represented by the pair (r,s).

7. The sender sends (m,r,s).

8. The receiver verifies the signature as follows:

   a. Compute:

   $$w=s^{-1} \bmod q$$

   $$u1=(\text{SHA1}(m)*w) \bmod q$$

   $$u2=(rw) \bmod q$$

   $$v=((g^{u1}y^{u2}) \bmod p) \bmod q$$

9. If v=r, then the signature is verified.

The above description shows the principles of using the hash functions in IPSec. Details such as what fields to include in the calculations and how are omitted. See Chapter 3, "Description of IPSec" on page 47 for a thorough presentation of the inner workings of IPSec.

2.5 Digital Certificates and Certification Authorities

As we said before in 2.3.1, "Authentication and Non-Repudiation" on page 32, with public-key cryptography, the parties retrieve each other's public key. There are security exposures here. An intruder could change some real public keys with his or her own public key, and then mount a so-called *man-in-the-middle attack*. It works like this. The intruder places himself between Alice and Bob. He can trick Bob by sending him one of his own public keys as if it were Alice's. The same applies to Alice. She thinks she uses Bob's public key, but the sour reality is that she actually uses the intruder's. So the clever intruder can decrypt the confidential traffic between the two and remain undetected. For example, a message sent by Alice and encrypted with "Bob's" public key lands at the intruder, who decrypts it, learns its content, then re-encrypts it with Bob's real public key. Bob has no way to realize that Alice is using a phony public key.

An intruder could also use impersonation, claiming to be somebody else, for example an online shopping mall, fouling innocent shoppers.

The solution to these serious threats is the *digital certificate*. A digital certificate is a file that binds an identity to the associated public key. This binding is validated by a trusted third party, the *certification authority (CA)*. A digital certificate is signed with the private key of the certification authority, so it can be authenticated. It is only issued after a verification of the applicant. Apart from the public key and identification, a digital certificate usually contains other information too, such as:

- Date of issue
- Expiry date
- Miscellaneous information from issuing CA (for example, serial number)

Note: There is an international standard in place for digital certificates: the ISO X.509 protocols.

Now the picture looks different. The parties retrieve each other's digital certificate and authenticate it using the public key of the issuing certification authority. They have confidence that the public keys are real, because a trusted third party vouches for them. The malicious online shopping mall is put out of business.

It easy to imagine that one CA can not cover all needs. What happens when Bob's certificate is issued by a CA unknown to Alice? Can she trust that unknown authority? Well, this is entirely her decision, but to make life easier, CAs can form a hierarchy, often referred to as the *trust chain*. Each member in the chain has a certificate signed by it superior authority. The higher the CA is in the chain, the tighter security procedures are in place. The root CA is trusted by everyone and its private key is top secret.

Alice can traverse the chain upwards until she finds a CA that she trusts. The traversal consists of verifying the subordinate CA's public key and identity using the certificate issued to it by the superior CA.

When a trusted CA is found up in the chain, Alice is assured that Bob's issuing CA is trustworthy. In fact this is all about delegation of trust. We trust your identity card if somebody who we trust signs it. And if the signer is unknown to us, we can go upward and see who signs for the signer, etc.

An implementation of this concept can be found in the SET protocol, where the major credit card brands operate their own CA hierarchies that converge to a common root. Lotus Notes authentication, as another example, is also based on certificates, and it can be implemented using hierarchical trust chains. PGP also uses a similar approach, but its trust chain is based on persons and it is rather a distributed Web than a strict hierarchical tree.

2.5.1 Usage of Digital Certificates with IPSec

IPSec uses digital certificates in the ISAKMP negotiations, for the following authentication modes:

- Digital signature (DSS)
- RSA encryption
- RSA signature

An IPSec certificate has a named subject (the identity), which could be any of the following:

- IP address
- IP address range
- Subnet address
- Domain name
- Fully qualified domain name
- Distinguished name
- Text string

Please refer to Chapter 4, "The Internet Key Exchange (IKE) Protocol" on page 71 for a more detailed description of ISAKMP/Oakley.

2.6 Random-Number Generators

An important component of a cryptosystem is the random-number generator. Many times random session keys and random initialization variables (often referred to as initialization vectors) are generated. For example, DES requires an explicit initialization vector and Diffie-Hellman relies on picking random numbers which serve as input for the key derivation.

The quality, that is the randomness of these generators, is more important than you would think. The ordinary random function provided with most programming language libraries is good enough for games, but not for cryptography. Those random-number generators are rather predictable; if you rely on them, be prepared for happy cryptanalysts finding interesting correlations in your encrypted output.

The fundamental problem faced by the random-number generators is that the computers are ultimately deterministic machines, so real random sequences cannot be produced. As John von Neumann ironically said: "Anyone who considers arithmetical methods of producing random digits is, of course, in a state of sin". (Quoted by Donald Knuth.) That's why the term *pseudorandom generator* is more appropriate.

Cryptographically strong pseudorandom generators must be unpredictable. It must be computationally infeasible to determine the next random bit, even with total knowledge of the generator.

A common practical solution for pseudorandom generators is to use hash functions. This approach provides sufficient randomness and it can be efficiently implemented. Military-grade generators use specialized devices that exploit the inherent randomness in physical phenomena. An interesting solution can be found in the PGP software. The initial seed of the pseudorandom generator is derived from measuring the time elapsed between the keystrokes of the user.

Note: The IPSec specifications state that a strong random-number generator must be used for initialization vector and key generation.

2.7 Export/Import Restrictions on Cryptography

U.S. export regulations changed in 1996, which put cryptography under the control of the Commerce Department. It had formerly been treated as a munition. This is a significant step in liberalizing the export of cryptographic products.

According to the new export regulations a license may be granted to export a 56-bit key encryption algorithm if a company has an approved key recovery plan. The key recovery plan must be implemented in 2 years and the license is granted on a 6 month basis.

In 1997 IBM was granted the license to export DES as long as it was used similarly to other products that have been approved. Recently, the export of triple-DES has been allowed for banking applications.

In September 1998, the White House announced further liberalization of U.S. export restrictions on cryptographic material and key recovery requirements which can be sumarized as follows:

- The key recovery requirement for export of 56-bit DES and equivalent products is eliminated. This includes products that use 1024-bit asymmetric key exchanges together with 56-bit symmetric key algorithms.

- Export of unlimited strength encryption (for example, 3DES) under license exceptions (with or without key recovery) is now broadened to include others besides the financial industry for 45 countries. This includes subsidiaries of U.S firms, insurance, health and medical (excluding biochemical and pharmaceutical manufacturers), and online merchants for the purpose of securing online transactions (excluding distributors of items considered munitions).

  For the latter, revocerable products will be granted exceptions world wide (excluding terrorist countries) without requiring a review of foreign key recovery agents.

- Export of recoverable products will be granted to most most commercial firms for a broad range of countries in the major commercial markets (excluding items on the U.S. munitions list).

- Export licenses to end users may be granted on a case-by-case basis.

These regulations are expected to be formally published by the U.S. Export Regulation Office in November 1998.

In France, according to the law, any product capable of enciphering/deciphering user data should be granted a license from the French government before being marketed. Then customers need to be authorized to use them on a case-by-case basis. In reality, two major and useful exceptions exist:

1. Routinely, licenses are granted that allow banks to use DES products on a global basis (no case-by-case authorization required).
2. Routinely, global licenses are granted that allow anybody to use weak encryption (RC2/RC4 with 40-bit keys).

Chapter 3. Description of IPSec

In this chapter we examine in detail the IPSec framework, its two main protocols, Authentication Header (AH) and Encapsulating Security Payload (ESP). The header formats, the specific cryptographic features and the different modes of application of AH and ESP are discussed.

Note: The third IPSec component, the Internet Key Exchange (IKE), formerly referred to as ISAKMP/Oakley, is mentioned briefly in Chapter 4, "The Internet Key Exchange (IKE) Protocol" on page 71. This decision is based upon the currently available IBM IPSec implementations that do no yet support IKE. IKE and its support within IBM products are discussed in detail in a separate redbook to be published early next year.

IPSec was designed for interoperability. When correctly implemented, it does not affect networks and hosts that do not support it. IPSec is independent of the current cryptographic algorithms; it can accommodate new ones as they become available. It works both with IPv4 and IPv6. Actually IPSec is a mandatory component of IPv6.

IPSec uses state-of-the-art cryptographic algorithms. The specific implementation of an algorithm for use by an IPSec protocol is often called a *transform*. For example, the DES algorithm used in ESP is called the ESP DES-CBC transform. The transforms, as the protocols, are published in RFCs and in Internet Drafts.

Note: Internet Drafts are working documents and are valid for a maximum of 6 months. You should check the Internet Engineering Task Force document repository (`http://www.ietf.org/home.html`) or another up-to-date repository for the latest drafts.

3.1 Concepts

Two major IPSec concepts should be clarified before entering the details: the Security Associations and the tunneling. In fact they are not new; IPSec just makes use of them. These concepts are described in the following sections.

3.1.1 Security Associations

The concept of a Security Association (SA) is fundamental to IPSec. An SA is a unidirectional (simplex) logical connection between two IPSec systems, uniquely identified by the following triple:

```
<Security Parameter Index, IP Destination Address, Security Protocol>
```

The definition of the members is as follows:

Security Parameter Index (SPI)
> This is a 32-bit value used to identify different SAs with the same destination address and security protocol. The SPI is carried in the header of the security protocol (AH or ESP). The SPI has only local significance, as defined by the creator of the SA. The SPI values in the range 1 to 255 are reserved by the Internet Assigned Numbers Authority (IANA). The SPI value of 0 must be used for local implementation-specific purposes only. Generally the SPI is selected by the destination system during the SA establishment.

IP Destination Address
> This address may be a unicast, broadcast or multicast address. However, currently SA management mechanisms are defined only for unicast addresses.

Security Protocol
> This can be either AH or ESP.

An SA can be in either of two modes: transport or tunnel, depending on the mode of the protocol in that SA. You can find the explanation of these protocol modes later in this chapter.

Because SAs are simplex, for bidirectional communication between two IPSec systems, there must be two SAs defined, one in each direction.

An SA gives security services to the traffic carried by it either by using AH or ESP, but not both. In other words, for a connection that should be protected by both AH and ESP, two SAs must be defined for each direction. In this case, the set of SAs that define the connection is referred to as an *SA bundle*. The SAs in the bundle do not have to terminate at the same endpoint. For example, a mobile host could use an AH SA between itself and a firewall and a nested ESP SA that extends to a host behind the firewall.

An IPSec implementation maintains two databases related to SAs:

Security Policy Database (SPD)
> The Security Policy Database specifies what security services are to be offered to the IP traffic, depending on factors such as source, destination, whether it is inbound, outbound, etc. It contains an ordered list of policy entries, separate for inbound and/or outbound traffic. These entries might specify that some traffic must not go through IPSec processing, some must be discarded and the rest must be processed by the IPSec module. Entries in this database are similar to the firewall rules or packet filters.

Security Association Database (SAD)

The Security Association Database contains parameter information about each SA, such as AH or ESP algorithms and keys, sequence numbers, protocol mode and SA lifetime. For outbound processing, an SPD entry points to an entry in the SAD. That is, the SPD determines which SA is to be used for a given packet. For inbound processing, the SAD is consulted to determine how the packet must be processed.

Notes:

1. The user interface of an IPSec implementation usually hides or presents in a more friendly way these databases and makes the life of the administrator easier.

2. IPSec policies will be discussed in more detail in the previously mentioned redbook about IKE, to be published at a later time.

3.1.2 Tunneling

Tunneling or encapsulation is a common technique in packet-switched networks. It consists of wrapping a packet in a new one. That is, a new header is attached to the original packet. The entire original packet becomes the payload of the new one, as it is shown in Figure 18.

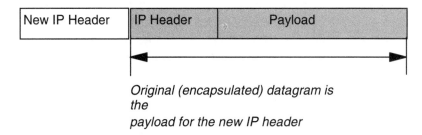

Figure 18. IP Tunneling

In general tunneling is used to carry traffic of one protocol over a network that does not support that protocol directly. For example, NetBIOS or IPX can be encapsulated in IP to carry it over a TCP/IP WAN link. In the case of IPSec, IP is tunneled through IP for a slightly different purpose: to provide total protection, including the header of the encapsulated packet. If the encapsulated packet is encrypted, an intruder cannot figure out for example the destination address of that packet. (Without tunneling he or she could.) The internal structure of a private network can be concealed in this way.

Tunneling requires intermediate processing of the original packet on its route. The destination specified in the outer header, usually an IPSec firewall or router, retrieves the original packet and sends it to the ultimate destination. The processing overhead is compensated by the extra security.

A notable advantage of IP tunneling is the possibility to exchange packets with private IP addresses between two intranets over the public Internet, which requires globally unique addresses. Since the encapsulated header is not processed by the Internet routers, only the endpoints of the tunnel (the gateways) have to have globally assigned addresses; the hosts in the intranets behind them can be assigned private addresses, for example 10.x.x.x. As globally unique IP addresses are becoming a scarce resource, this interconnection method gains importance.

Note: IPSec tunneling is modeled after RFC 2003 *IP Encapsulation within IP*. It was originally designed for Mobile IP, an architecture that allows a mobile host to keep its home IP address even if attached to remote or foreign subnets.

3.1.3 Terminology Used throughout IPSec Redbooks

IPSec is a relatively new technology and it has a less coherent terminology than IP in general. In this section we summarize how the IPSec terms are used by us.

Gateway, Router and Firewall
> Although these are separate entities, often they can be used interchangeably when the IPSec functionality is in focus. Usually we use the term gateway to denote a machine which routes IP traffic, as opposed to a host, which generates or consumes that traffic. The term *security gateway* is analogous. It is more precise since the name implies that the box is IPSec-capable.

IPSec Tunnel
> This term is used to denote a pair of SAs that realize a bidirectional connection between two IPSec systems. It does not imply either transport or tunnel mode. Sometimes it is called simply a *tunnel*.

Selectors
> Selectors define the IPSec processing of the outbound packets. The SPD entries consist of one or more selectors.

Packet Filters
> These are rules that steer traffic into or out of the tunnel. The traffic might be either inbound or outbound.

3.2 Authentication Header (AH)

AH is used to provide integrity and authentication to IP datagrams. Optional replay protection is also possible. Although its usage is optional, the replay protection service must be implemented by any IPSec-compliant system. The mentioned services are connectionless; that is they work on a per-packet basis.

AH authenticates as much of the IP datagram as possible. Some fields in the IP header change en-route and their value cannot be predicted by the receiver. These fields are called *mutable* and are not protected by AH. The mutable IPv4 fields are:

- Type of Service (TOS)
- Flags
- Fragment Offset
- Time to Live (TTL)
- Header Checksum

When protection of these fields is required, tunneling should be used. The payload of the IP packet is considered immutable and is always protected by AH.

AH is identified by protocol number 51, assigned by the IANA. The protocol header (IPv4, IPv6, or Extension) immediately preceding the AH header contains this value in its Protocol (IPv4) or Next Header (IPv6, Extension) field.

AH processing is applied only to non-fragmented IP packets. However an IP packet with AH applied can be fragmented by intermediate routers. In this case the destination first reassembles the packet and then applies AH processing to it. If an IP packet that appears to be a fragment (offset field is non-zero, or the More Fragments bit is set) is input to AH processing, it is discarded. This prevents the so-called *overlapping fragment attack*, which misuses the fragment reassembly algorithm in order to create forged packets and force them through a firewall.

Packets that failed authentication are discarded and never delivered to upper layers. This mode of operation greatly reduces the chances of successful *denial of service* attacks, which aim to block the communication of a host or gateway by flooding it with bogus packets.

3.2.1 AH Header Format

The current AH header format is described in the Internet Draft *draft-ietf-ipsec-auth-header-07.txt*, which contains important modifications compared to the previous AH specification, RFC 1826. The information in this section is based on the respective Internet Draft.

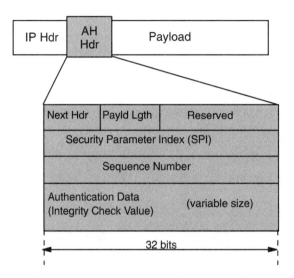

Figure 19. AH Header Format

In Figure 19 the position of the AH header in the IP packet and the header fields are shown. The explanation of the fields are as follows:

Next Header
> The Next Header is an 8-bit field that identifies the type of the next payload after the Authentication Header. The value of this field is chosen from the set of IP protocol numbers defined in the most recent *Assigned Numbers* RFC from the Internet Assigned Numbers Authority (IANA).

Payload Length
> This field is 8 bits long and contains the length of the AH header expressed in 32-bit words, minus 2. It does not relate to the actual payload length of the IP packet as a whole. If default options are used, the value is 4 (three 32-bit fixed words plus three 32-bit words of authentication data minus two).

Reserved
> This field is reserved for future use. Its length is 16 bits and it is set to zero.

Security Parameter Index (SPI)

This field is 32 bits in length. See Security Parameter Index (SPI) on page 48 for a definition.

Sequence Number

This 32-bit field is a monotonically increasing counter which is used for replay protection. Replay protection is optional; however, this field is mandatory. The sender always includes this field and it is at the discretion of the receiver to process it or not. At the establishment of an SA the sequence number is initialized to zero. The first packet transmitted using the SA has a sequence number of 1. Sequence numbers are not allowed to repeat. Thus the maximum number of IP packets that can be transmitted on any given SA is $2^{32}-1$. After the highest sequence number is used, a new SA and consequently a new key is established. Anti-replay is enabled at the sender by default. If upon SA establishment the receiver chooses not to use it, the sender does not concern with the value in this field anymore.

Notes:

1. Typically the anti-replay mechanism is not used with manual key management.

2. The original AH specification in RFC 1826 did not discuss the concept of sequence numbers. Older IPSec implementations that are based on that RFC can therefore not provide replay protection.

Authentication Data

This is a variable-length field, also called Integrity Check Value (ICV). The ICV for the packet is calculated with the algorithm selected at the SA initialization. The authentication data length is an integral multiple of 32 bits. As its name tells, it is used by the receiver to verify the integrity of the incoming packet.

In theory any MAC algorithm can be used to calculate the ICV. The specification requires that HMAC-MD5-96 and HMAC-SHA-1-96 must be supported. The old RFC 1826 requires Keyed MD5. In practice Keyed SHA-1 is also used. Implementations usually support two to four algorithms.

When doing the ICV calculation, the mutable fields are considered to be filled with zero.

3.2.2 Ways of Using AH

AH can be used in two ways: transport mode and tunnel mode.

3.2.2.1 AH in Transport Mode

In this mode the original IP datagram is taken and the AH header is inserted right after the IP header, as shown in Figure 20. If the datagram already has IPSec header(s), then the AH header is inserted before any of those.

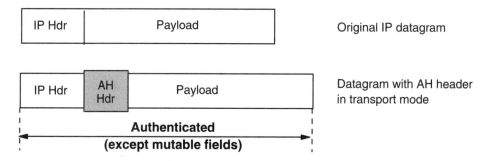

Figure 20. *Authentication Header in Transport Mode*

The transport mode is used by hosts, not by gateways. Gateways are not even required to support transport mode.

The advantage of the transport mode is less processing overhead. The disadvantage is that the mutable fields are not authenticated.

3.2.2.2 AH in Tunnel Mode

With this mode the tunneling concept is applied a new IP datagram is constructed and the original IP datagram is made the payload of it. Then AH in transport mode is applied to the resulting datagram. See Figure 21 on page 55 for an illustration.

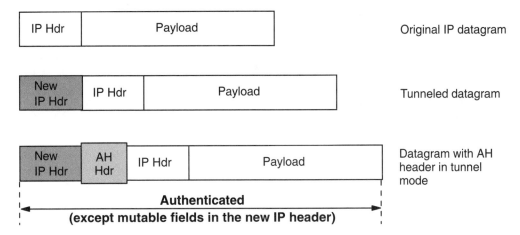

Figure 21. Authentication Header in Tunnel Mode

The tunnel mode is used whenever either end of a security association is a gateway. Thus, between two firewalls the tunnel mode is always used.

Although gateways are supposed to support tunnel mode only, often they can also work in transport mode. This mode is allowed when the gateway acts as a host, that is in cases when traffic is destined to itself. Examples are SNMP commands or ICMP echo requests.

In tunnel mode the outer headers' IP addresses does not need to be the same as the inner headers' addresses. For example two security gateways may operate an AH tunnel which is used to authenticate all traffic between the networks they connect together. This is a very typical mode of operation. Hosts are not required to support tunnel mode, but often they do.

The advantages of the tunnel mode are total protection of the encapsulated IP datagram and the possibility of using private addresses. However, there is an extra processing overhead associated with this mode.

Note: The original AH specification in RFC 1825 only mentions tunnel mode in passing, not as a requirement. Because of this, there are IPSec implementations based on that RFC that do not support AH in tunnel mode. This has implications in the ability to implement certain scenarios, such as the one described in Chapter 7, "Remote Access Scenario" on page 111.

3.2.3 IPv6 Considerations

AH is an integral part of IPv6. In an IPv6 environment, AH is considered an
end-to-end payload and it appears after hop-by-hop, routing, and fragmentation
extension headers. The destination options extension header(s) could appear either
before or after the AH header. Figure 22 illustrates the positioning of the AH header
in transport mode for a typical IPv6 packet. The position of the extension headers
marked with * is variable, if present at all.

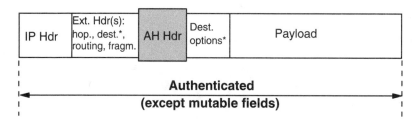

Figure 22. AH in Transport Mode for IPv6

For a detailed description of AH in IPv6 please refer to the current Internet Draft.

3.3 Encapsulating Security Payload (ESP)

ESP is used to provide integrity check, authentication and encryption to IP datagrams.
Optional replay protection is also possible. These services are connectionless; they
operate on a per-packet basis. The set of desired services are selectable upon SA
establishment. However, some restrictions apply:

- Integrity check and authentication go together

- Replay protection is selectable only with integrity check and authentication

- Replay protection can be selected only by the receiver

Encryption is selectable independent of the other services. It is highly recommended
that if encryption is enabled, then integrity check and authentication be turned on. If
only encryption is used, intruders could forge packets in order to mount cryptanalytic
attacks. This is infeasible when integrity check and authentication are in place.

Although both authentication (with integrity check) and encryption are optional, at
least one of them is always selected. Otherwise it really does not make sense to use
ESP at all.

ESP is identified by protocol number 50, assigned by the IANA. The protocol header (IPv4, IPv6, or Extension) immediately preceding the AH header will contain this value in its Protocol (IPv4) or Next Header (IPv6, Extension) field.

ESP processing is applied only to non-fragmented IP packets. However an IP packet with ESP applied can be fragmented by intermediate routers. In this case the destination first reassembles the packet and then applies ESP processing to it. If an IP packet that appears to be a fragment (offset field is non-zero, or the More Fragments bit is set) is input to ESP processing, it is discarded. This prevents the overlapping fragment attack mentioned in 3.2, "Authentication Header (AH)" on page 51.

If both encryption and authentication with integrity check are selected, then the receiver first authenticates the packet and only if this step was successful proceeds with decryption. This mode of operation saves computing resources and reduces the vulnerability to denial of service attacks.

3.3.1 ESP Packet Format

The current ESP packet format is described in the Internet Draft *draft-ietf-ipsec-esp-v2-06.txt*, dated March 1998. It contains important modifications compared to the previous ESP specification, RFC 1827. The information in this section is based on the respective Internet Draft.

The format of the ESP packet is more complicated than that of the AH packet. Actually there is not only an ESP header, but also an ESP trailer and ESP authentication data (see Figure 23 on page 58). The payload is located (*encapsulated*) between the header and the trailer, hence the name of the the protocol.

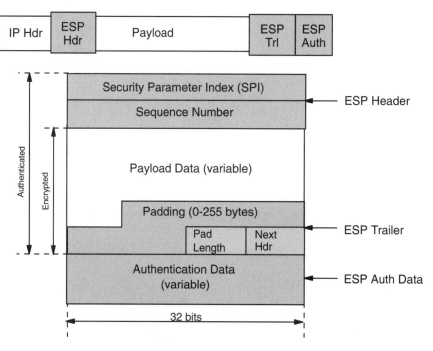

Figure 23. ESP Header and Trailer

The following fields are part of an ESP packet:

Security Parameter Index (SPI)
> This field is 32 bits in length. See Security Parameter Index (SPI) on page 48 for the definition.

Sequence Number
> This 32-bit field is a monotonically increasing counter. See Sequence Number on page 53 for the definition.

> **Notes:**

> 1. Typically the anti-replay mechanism is not used with manual key management.

> 2. The original ESP specification in RFC 1827 did not discuss the concept of sequence numbers. Older IPSec implementations that are based on that RFC can therefore not provide replay protection.

Payload Data
> The Payload Data field is mandatory. It consists of a variable number of bytes of data described by the Next Header field. This field is encrypted with the

cryptographic algorithm selected during SA establishment. If the algorithm requires initialization vectors, these are also included here.

The ESP specification require support for the DES algorithm in CBC mode (DES-CBC transform). Often other encryption algorithms are also supported, such as triple-DES and CDMF in the case of IBM products.

Padding

Most encryption algorithms require that the input data must be an integral number of blocks. Also, the resulting ciphertext (including the Padding, Pad Length and Next Header fields) must terminate on a 4-byte boundary, so that Next Header field is right-aligned. That's why this variable length field is included. It can be used to hide the length of the original messages too. However, this could adversely impact the effective bandwidth. Padding is an optional field.

Note: The encryption covers the Payload Data, Padding, Pad Length and Next Header fields.

Pad Length

This 8-bit field contains the number of the preceding padding bytes. It is always present, and the value of 0 indicates no padding.

Next Header

The Next Header is an 8-bit mandatory field that shows the data type carried in the payload, for example an upper-level protocol identifier such as TCP. The values are chosen from the set of IP protocol numbers defined by the IANA.

Authentication Data

This field is variable in length and contains the ICV calculated for the ESP packet from the SPI to the Next Header field inclusive. The Authentication Data field is optional. It is included only when integrity check and authentication have been selected at SA initialization time.

The ESP specifications require two authentication algorithms to be supported: HMAC with MD5 and HMAC with SHA-1. Often the simpler keyed versions are also supported by the IPSec implementations.

Notes:

1. The IP header is not covered by the ICV.

2. The original ESP specification in RFC 1827 discusses the concept of authentication within ESP in conjunction with the encryption transform. That is, there is no Authentication Data field and it is left to the encryption transforms to eventually provide authentication.

3.3.2 Ways of Using ESP

Like AH, ESP can be used in two ways: transport mode and tunnel mode.

3.3.2.1 ESP in Transport Mode

In this mode the original IP datagram is taken and the ESP header is inserted right after the IP header, as it is shown in Figure 24. If the datagram already has IPSec header(s), then the ESP header is inserted before any of those. The ESP trailer and the optional authentication data are appended to the payload.

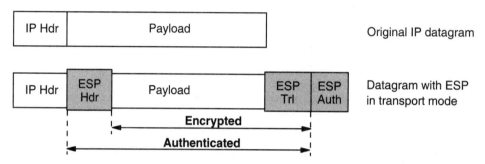

Figure 24. ESP in Transport Mode

ESP in transport mode provides neither authentication nor encryption for the IP header. This is a disadvantage, since false packets might be delivered for ESP processing. The advantage of transport mode is the lower processing overhead.

As in the case of AH, ESP in transport mode is used by hosts, not gateways. Gateways are not even required to support transport mode.

3.3.2.2 ESP in Tunnel Mode

As expected, this mode applies the tunneling principle. A new IP packet is constructed with a new IP header and then ESP in transport mode is applied, as illustrated in Figure 25 on page 61. Since the original datagram becomes the payload data for the new ESP packet, its protection is total if both encryption and authentication are selected. However, the new IP header is still not protected.

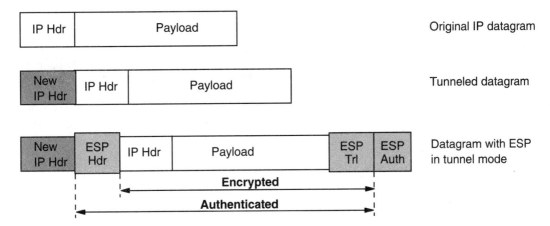

Figure 25. ESP in Tunnel Mode

The tunnel mode is used whenever either end of a security association is a gateway. Thus, between two firewalls the tunnel mode is always used.

Although gateways are supposed to support tunnel mode only, often they can also work in transport mode. This mode is allowed when the gateway acts as a host, that is in cases when traffic is destined to itself. Examples are SNMP commands or ICMP echo requests.

In tunnel mode the outer headers' IP addresses does not need to be the same as the inner headers' addresses. For example two security gateways may operate an ESP tunnel which is used to secure all traffic between the networks they connect together. Hosts are not required to support tunnel mode, but often they do.

The advantages of the tunnel mode are total protection of the encapsulated IP datagram and the possibility of using private addresses. However, there is an extra processing overhead associated with this mode.

3.3.3 IPv6 Considerations

Like AH, ESP is an integral part of IPv6. In an IPv6 environment, ESP is considered an end-to-end payload and it appears after hop-by-hop, routing, and fragmentation extension headers. The destination options extension header(s) could appear either before or after the AH header. Figure 26 on page 62 illustrates the positioning of the AH header in transport mode for a typical IPv6 packet. The position of the extension headers marked with * is variable, if present at all.

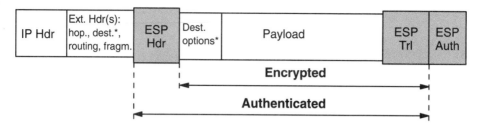

Figure 26. ESP in Transport Mode for IPv6

For more details, please refer to the respective Internet Draft.

3.3.4 Why Two Authentication Protocols?

Knowing about the security services of ESP, one might ask if there is really a requirement for AH. Why does ESP authentication not cover the IP header as well? There is no official answer to these questions, but here are some points that justify the existence of two different IPSec authentication protocols:

- ESP requires strong cryptographic algorithms to be implemented, whether it will actually be used or not. Strong cryptography is an over-hyped and sensitive topic in some countries, with restrictive regulations in place. It might be troublesome to deploy ESP-based solutions in such areas. However, authentication is not regulated and AH can be used freely around the world.

- Often only authentication is needed. While ESP could have been specified to cover the IP header as well, AH is more performant compared to ESP with authentication only, because of the simpler format and lower processing overhead. It makes sense to use AH in these cases.

- Having two different protocols means finer-grade control over an IPSec network and more flexible security options. By nesting AH and ESP for example, one can implement IPSec tunnels that combine the strengths of both protocols.

3.4 Combining IPSec Protocols

The AH and ESP protocols can be applied alone or in combination. Given the two modes of each protocol, there is quite a number of possible combinations. To make things even worse, the AH and ESP SAs do not need to have identical endpoints, so the picture becomes rather complicated. Luckily, out of the many possibilities only a few make sense in real-world scenarios.

Note: The *draft-ietf-ipsec-arch-sec-07.txt* Internet Draft is the current document that describes the mandatory combinations that must be supported by each IPSec implementation. Other combinations may also be supported, but this might impact interoperability.

We mentioned in 3.1.1, "Security Associations" on page 47 that the combinations of IPSec protocols are realized with SA bundles.

There are two approaches for an SA bundle creation:

- *Transport adjacency:* Both security protocols are applied in transport mode to the same IP datagram. This method is practical for only one level of combination.

- *Iterated (nested) tunneling:* The security protocols are applied in tunnel mode in sequence. After each application a new IP datagram is created and the next protocol is applied to it. This method has no limit in the nesting levels. However, more than three levels are impractical.

These approaches can be combined, for example an IP packet with transport adjacency IPSec headers can be sent through nested tunnels.

When designing a VPN, one should limit the IPSec processing stages applied to a certain packet to a reasonable level. In our view three applications is that limit over which further processing has no benefits. Two stages are sufficient for almost all the cases.

Note that in order to be able to create an SA bundle in which the SAs have different endpoints, at least one level of tunneling must be applied. Transport adjacency does not allow for multiple source/destination addresses, because only one IP header is present.

The practical principle of the combined usage is that upon the receipt of a packet with both protocol headers, the IPSec processing sequence should be authentication followed by decryption. It is a common sense decision not to bother with the decryption of packets of uncertain origin.

Following the above principle, the sender first applies ESP and then AH to the outbound traffic. In fact this sequence is an explicit requirement for transport mode IPSec processing. When using both ESP and AH, a new question arises: should ESP authentication be turned on? AH authenticates the packet anyway. The answer is simple. Turning ESP authentication on makes sense only when the ESP SA extends beyond the AH SA, as in the case of the supplier scenario. In this case, not only does it make sense to use ESP authentication, but it is highly recommended to do so, to avoid spoofing attacks in the intranet.

As far as the modes are concerned, the usual way is that transport mode is used between the endpoints of a connection and tunnel mode is used between two machines when at least one of them is a gateway.

Let's take a systematic look on the plausible ways of using the IPSec protocols, from the simplest to the more complicated nested setups.

3.4.1 Case 1: End-to-End Security

As shown in Figure 27, two hosts are connected through the Internet (or an intranet) without any IPSec gateway between them. They can use ESP, AH or both. Either transport or tunnel mode can be applied.

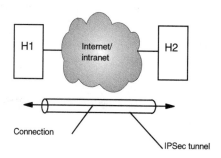

Figure 27. *End-to-End Security*

The combinations required to be supported by any IPSec implementation are the following:

Transport Mode

    1. AH alone
    2. ESP alone
    3. AH applied after ESP (transport adjacency)

Tunnel Mode

    1. AH alone
    2. ESP alone

3.4.2 Case 2: Basic VPN Support

Figure 28 on page 65 illustrates the simplest VPN. The gateways G1 and G2 run the IPSec protocol stack. The hosts in the intranets are not required to support IPSec.

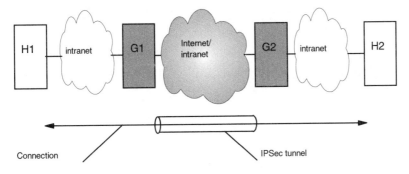

Figure 28. Basic VPN Support

In this case the gateways are required to support only tunnel mode, either with AH or ESP.

3.4.2.1 Combined Tunnels between Gateways

Although the gateways are required to support only an AH tunnel or ESP tunnel, often it is desirable to have tunnels between gateways that combine the features of both IPSec protocols.

The IBM IPSec implementations support this type of combined AH-ESP tunnels. The order of the headers is user selectable by setting the tunnel policy. (See A.1.1.2, "Policies" on page 119 for more details.)

A combined tunnel between the gateways does not mean that iterated tunneling takes place. Since the SA bundle comprising the tunnel have identical endpoints, it is inefficient to do iterated tunneling. Instead, one IPSec protocol is applied in tunnel mode and the other in transport mode, which can be conceptually thought of as a combined AH-ESP tunnel. An equivalent approach is to IP tunnel the original datagram and then apply transport adjacency IPSec processing to it. The result is that we have an outer IP header followed by the IPSec headers in the order set by the tunnel policy, then the original IP packet, as it is shown in the figure below. This is the packet format in a combined AH-ESP tunnel between two IBM firewalls.

Note: The ESP authentication data is not present because the IPSec implementation in the IBM firewall does not support the new specifications yet.

Outer IP Hdr	AH Hdr	ESP Hdr	Inner IP Hdr	Payload	ESP Trl

Figure 29. Combined AH-ESP Tunnel

3.4.3 Case 3: End-to-End Security with VPN Support

This case is a combination of cases 1 and 2 and it does not raise new IPSec requirements for the machines involved (see Figure 30). The big difference from case 2 is that now the hosts are also required to support IPSec.

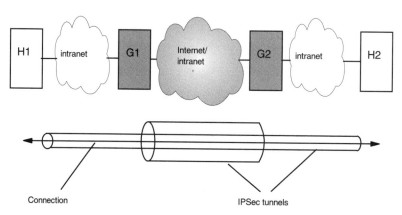

Figure 30. End-to-End Security with VPN Support

In a typical setup, the gateways use AH in tunnel mode, while the hosts use ESP in transport mode. An enhanced security version could use a combined AH-ESP tunnel between the gateways. In this way the ultimate destination addresses would be encrypted, the whole packet traveling the Internet would be authenticated and the carried data double encrypted. This is the only case when three stages of IPSec processing might be useful, however, at a cost; the performance impact is considerable.

3.4.4 Case 4: Remote Access

This case, shown in Figure 31 on page 67, applies to the remote hosts that use the Internet to reach a server in the organization protected by a firewall. The remote host commonly uses a PPP dial-in connection to an ISP.

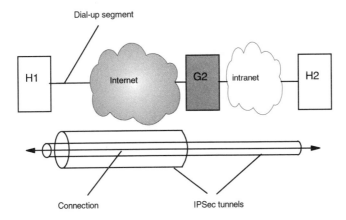

Figure 31. Remote Access

Between the remote host H1 and the firewall G2 only tunnel mode is required. The choices are the same as in case 2. Between the hosts themselves either tunnel mode or transport mode can be used, with the same choices as in case 1.

A typical setup is to use AH in tunnel mode between H1 and G2 and ESP in transport mode between H1 and H2. Older IPSec implementations that do not support AH in tunnel mode cannot implement this.

It is also common to create a combined AH-ESP tunnel between the remote host H1 and the gateway G2. In this case H1 can access the whole intranet with using just one SA bundle, whereas if it were using the setup shown in Figure 31, it only could access one host with one SA bundle.

3.4.5 Conclusion and an Example

While the combination of the IPSec protocols in theory leads to a large number of possibilities, in practice only a few (those presented above) are used. One very common combination is AH in tunnel mode protecting ESP traffic in transport mode. Combined AH-ESP tunnels between firewalls are also frequent.

Figure 32 on page 68 shows in detail how the first combination is realized. Consider that host H1 in Figure 30 on page 66 sends an IP packet to host H2. Here is what happens:

1. Host H1 constructs the IP packet and applies ESP transport to it. H1 then sends the datagram to gateway G1, the destination address being H2.

2. Gateway G1 realizes that this packet should be routed to G2. Upon consulting its IPSec databases (SPD and SAD) G1 concludes that AH in tunnel mode must be

applied before sending the packet out. It does the required encapsulation. Now the IP packet has the address of G2 as its destination, the ultimate destination H2 being encapsulated.

3. Gateway G2 receives the AH-tunneled packet. It is destined to itself, so it authenticates the datagram and strips off the outer header. G2 sees that the payload is yet another IP packet (that one sent by H1) with destination H2, so it forwards to H2. G2 does not care that this packet has an ESP header.

4. Finally H2 receives the packet. As this is the destination, ESP-transport processing is applied and the original payload retrieved.

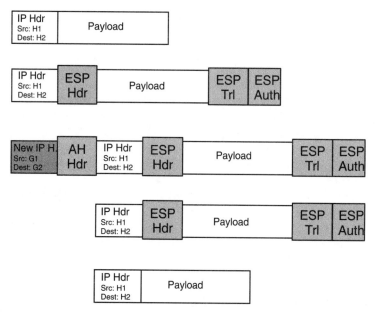

Figure 32. *Nesting of IPSec Protocols*

3.5 Current IPSec Standards and Internet Drafts

At the time of writing this book, publication of the following Internet Draft documents has been approved by the IETF as Proposed Standards but no RFC numbers have yet been assigned:

Security Architecture for the Internet Protocol
        http://www.ietf.org/internet-drafts/draft-ietf-ipsec-arch-sec-07.txt
IP Authentication Header (AH)
        http://www.ietf.org/internet-drafts/draft-ietf-ipsec-auth-header-07.txt

IP Encapsulating Security Payload (ESP)
        `http://www.ietf.org/internet-drafts/draft-ietf-ipsec-esp-v2-06.txt`
Internet Security Association and Key Management Protocol (ISAKMP)
        `http://www.ietf.org/internet-drafts/draft-ietf-ipsec-isakmp-10.txt`
Internet Key Exchange (IKE)
        `http://www.ietf.org/internet-drafts/draft-ietf-ipsec-isakmp-oakley-08.txt`
IPSec Domain of Interpretation for ISAKMP
        `http://www.ietf.org/internet-drafts/draft-ietf-ipsec-ipsec-doi-10.txt`
The Use of HMAC-MD5-96 within ESP and AH
        `http://www.ietf.org/internet-drafts/draft-ietf-ipsec-auth-hmac-md5-96-03.txt`
The Use of HMAC-SHA-1-96 within ESP and AH
        `http://www.ietf.org/internet-drafts/draft-ietf-ipsec-auth-hmac-sha196-03.txt`
The ESP DES-CBC Cipher Algorithm With Explicit IV
        `http://www.ietf.org/internet-drafts/draft-ietf-ipsec-ciph-des-expiv-02.txt`
The NULL Encryption Algorithm and Its Use With IPsec
        `http://www.ietf.org/internet-drafts/draft-ietf-ipsec-ciph-null-01.txt`

At the time of writing this book, publication of the following Internet Draft documents has been approved by the IETF as Informational RFCs but no RFC numbers have yet been assigned:

Oakley Key Determination Protocol
        `http://www.ietf.org/internet-drafts/draft-ietf-ipsec-oakley-02.txt`
IPSec Working Group to consider Security Document Roadmap
        `http://www.ietf.org/internet-drafts/draft-ietf-ipsec-doc-roadmap-02.txt`

Chapter 4. The Internet Key Exchange (IKE) Protocol

We have mentioned throughout previous chapters that the crucial elements of IPSec are Security Associations (SA) and the information that they provide in regard of identifying the partners of a secure communications channel, the cryptographic algorithms and keys to be used. You have also learned in 1.3.1.4, "ISAKMP/Oakley" on page 11 that the Internet Key Exchange (IKE) framework, also referred to as ISAKMP/Oakley, supports automated negotiation of Security Associations, and automated generation and refresh of cryptographic keys. The ability to perform these functions with little or no manual configuration of machines will be a critical element as a VPN grows in size.

As a reminder, we would like to repeat that secure exchange of keys is the most critical factor in establishing a secure communications environment. No matter how strong your authentication and encryption are, they are worthless if your key is compromised.

In this chapter, we introduce the concept and basic operation of ISAKMP/Oakley as defined in the current Internet Drafts. A detailed discussion of ISAKMP/Oakley and IBM implementations thereof will be provided in a separate IBM redbook to be published at a later time.

Before describing the details of the key exchange and update messages, some explanations are due:

Internet Security Association and Key Management Protocol (ISAKMP)
> A framework that defines the management of security associations (negotiate, modify, delete) and keys, and it also defines the payloads for exchanging key generation and authentication data. ISAKMP itself does not define any key exchange protocols, and the framework it provides can be applied to security mechanisms on the network, transport or application layer, and also to itself.

Oakley
> A key exchange protocol that can be used with the ISAKMP framework to exchange and update keying material for security associations.

Domain of Interpretation
> Definition of a set of protocols to be used with the ISAKMP framework for a particular environment, and a set of common definitions shared with those protocols regarding syntax of SA attributes and payload contents, namespace of

cryptographic transforms, etc. In relation to IPSec, the DOI instantiates ISAKMP for use with IP.

Internet Key Exchange (IKE)

A protocol that uses parts of ISAKMP and parts of the Oakley and SKEME key exchange protocols to provide management of keys and security associations for the IPSec AH and ESP protocols, and for ISAKMP itself.

4.1 Protocol Overview

ISAKMP requires that all information exchanges must be both encrypted and authenticated so that no one can eavesdrop on the keying material, and the keying material will be exchanged only among authenticated parties. This is required because the ISAKMP procedures deal with initializing the keys, so they must be capable of running over links where no security can be assumed to exist. Hence, the ISAKMP protocols use the most complex and processor-intensive operations in the IPSec protocol suite.

In addition, the ISAKMP methods have been designed with the explicit goals of providing protection against several well-known exposures:

- Denial-of-Service: The messages are constructed with unique *cookies* that can be used to quickly identify and reject invalid messages without the need to execute processor-intensive cryptographic operations.

- Man-in-the-Middle: Protection is provided against the common attacks such as deletion of messages, modification of messages, reflecting messages back to the sender, replaying of old messages, and redirection of messages to unintended recipients.

- Perfect Forward Secrecy (PFS): Compromise of past keys provides no useful clues for breaking any other key, whether it occurred before or after the compromised key. That is, each refreshed key will be derived without any dependence on predecessor keys.

The following authentication methods are defined for IKE:

1. Pre-shared key

2. Digital sigantures (DSS and RSA)

3. Public key encryption (RSA and revised RSA)

4.1.1 The Two Phases of ISAKMP/Oakley

The robustness of any cryptography-based solution depends much more strongly on keeping the keys secret than it does on the actual details of the chosen cryptographic algorithms. Hence, the IETF IPSec Working Group has prescribed a set of extremely robust ISAKMP/Oakley exchange protocols. It uses a 2-phase approach:

1. **Phase 1:** This set of negotiations establishes a master secret from which all cryptographic keys will subsequently be derived for protecting the users' data traffic. In the most general case, public key cryptography is used to establish an ISAKMP security association between systems, and to establish the keys that will be used to protect the ISAKMP messages that will flow in the subsequent Phase 2 negotiations. Phase 1 is concerned only with establishing the protection suite for the ISAKMP messages themselves, but it does not establish any security associations or keys for protecting user data.

   In Phase 1, the cryptographic operations are the most processor-intensive but need only be done infrequently, and a single Phase 1 exchange can be used to support multiple subsequent Phase 2 exchanges. As a rule of thumb, Phase 1 negotiations are executed once a day or maybe once a week, while Phase 2 negotiations are executed once every few minutes.

2. **Phase 2:** Phase 2 exchanges are less complex, since they are used only after the security protection suite negotiated in Phase 1 has been activated. A set of communicating systems negotiate the security associations and keys that will protect user data exchanges. Phase 2 ISAKMP messages are protected by the ISAKMP security association generated in Phase 1. Phase 2 negotiations generally occur more frequently than Phase 1. For example, a typical application of a Phase 2 negotiation is to refresh the cryptographic keys once every two to three minutes.

An illustration of the use of ISAKMP/Oakley to initially establish security associations and exchange keys between two systems is given in 4.2, "Initializing Security Associations with ISAKMP/Oakley" on page 74.

But the ISAKMP protocol offers a solution even when the remote host's IP address is not known in advance. ISAKMP allows a remote host to identify itself by a *permanent* identifier, such as a name or an e-mail address. The ISAKMP Phase 1 exchanges will then authenticate the remote host's permanent identity using public key cryptography:

- Certificates create a binding between the permanent identifier and a public key. Therefore, ISAKMP's certificate-based Phase 1 message exchanges can authenticate the remote host's permanent identify.

- Since the ISAKMP messages themselves are carried within IP datagrams, the ISAKMP partner (for example, a firewall or destination host) can associate the remote host's dynamic IP address with its authenticated permanent identity.

See 4.2, "Initializing Security Associations with ISAKMP/Oakley" for a detailed discussion of how ISAKMP/Oakley exchanges authenticate the remote host to its peer and set up the security associations dictated by its corporate VPN policy.

4.2 Initializing Security Associations with ISAKMP/Oakley

This section outlines how ISAKMP/Oakley protocols initially establish security associations and exchange keys between two systems that wish to communicate securely.

In the remainder of this section, we assume that the parties involved are named Host-A and Host-B. Host-A will be the initiator of the ISAKMP Phase 1 exchanges, and Host-B will be the responder. If needed for clarity, subscripts A or B will be used to identify the source of various fields in the message exchanges.

4.2.1 Phase 1 - Setting Up the ISAKMP Security Associations

The security associations that protect the ISAKMP messages themselves are set up during the Phase 1 exchanges. Since we are starting "cold" (no previous keys or SAs have been negotiated between Host-A and Host-B), the Phase 1 exchanges will use the ISAKMP Identity Protect exchange (also known as Oakley Main Mode). Six messages are needed to complete the exchange:

- Messages 1 and 2 negotiate the characteristics of the security associations. Messages 1 and 2 flow in the clear for the initial Phase 1 exchange, and they are unauthenticated.
- Messages 3 and 4 exchange nonces (random values) and also execute a Diffie-Hellman exchange to establish a master key (SKEYID). Messages 3 and 4 flow in the clear for the initial Phase 1 exchange, and they are unauthenticated.
- Messages 5 and 6 exchange the required information for mutually authenticating the parties' identities. The payloads of Messages 5 and 6 are protected by the encryption algorithm and keying material established with messages 1 through 4.

The detailed description of the Phase 1 messages and exchanged information follows below:

4.2.1.1 IKE Phase 1, Message 1

Since Host-A is the initiating party, it will construct a cleartext ISAKMP message (Message 1) and send it to Host-B. The ISAKMP message itself is carried as the payload of a UDP packet, which in turn is carried as the payload of a normal IP datagram (see Figure 33).

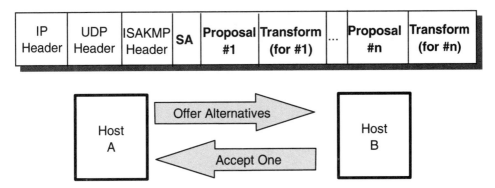

Figure 33. Message 1 of an ISAKMP Phase 1 Exchange

The source and destination addresses to be placed in the IP header are those of Host-A (initiator) and Host-B (responder), respectively. The UDP header will identify that the destination port is 500, which has been assigned for use by the ISAKMP protocol. The payload of the UDP packet carries the ISAKMP message itself.

In Message 1, Host-A, the initiator, proposes a set of one or more protection suites for consideration by Host-B, the responder. Hence, the ISAKMP Message contains at least the following fields in its payload:

ISAKMP Header
> The ISAKMP Header in Message 1 will indicate an exchange type of Main Mode, and will contain a Message ID of 0. Host-A will set the Responder Cookie field to 0, and will fill in a random value of its choice for the Initiator Cookie, denoted as Cookie-A.

Security Association
> The Security Association field identifies the Domain of Interpretation (DOI). Since the hosts plan to run IPSec protocols between themselves, the DOI is simply IP.

Proposal Payload
> Host-A's Proposal Payload will specify the protocol PROTO_ISAKMP and will set the SPI value to 0.

Note: For ISAKMP Phase 1 messages, the actual SPI field within the Proposal Payload is not used to identify the ISAKMP Security Association. During Phase 1, the ISAKMP SA is identified instead by the pair of values <Initiator Cookie, Responder Cookie>, both of which must be non-zero values. Since the Responder Cookie has not yet been generated by Host-B, the ISAKMP SA is not yet unambiguously identified.

Transform Payload

The Transform Payload will specify KEY_OAKLEY. For the KEY_OAKLEY transform, Host-A must also specify the relevant attributes: namely, the authentication method to be used, the pseudo-random function to be used, and the encryption algorithm to be used.

Note: Multiple proposals can be included in Message 1.

4.2.1.2 IKE Phase 1, Message 2

In Message 1, Host-A proposed one or more candidate protection suites to be used to protect the ISAKMP exchanges. Host-B uses Message 2 to indicate which one, if any, it will support. If Host-A proposed just a single option, Host-B merely needs to acknowledge that the proposal is acceptable.

The source and destination addresses to be placed in the IP header are those of Host-B (responder) and Host-A (initiator), respectively. The UDP header will identify that the destination port is 500, which has been assigned for use by the ISAKMP protocol. The payload of the UDP packet carries the ISAKMP message itself.

The message contents will be as follows:

ISAKMP Header

The ISAKMP Header in Message 2 will indicate an exchange type of Main Mode, and will contain a Message ID of 0. Host-B will set the Responder Cookie field to a random value, which we will call Cookie-B, and will copy into the Initiator Cookie field the value that was received in the Cookie-A field of Message 1. The value pair <Cookie-A, Cookie-B> will serve as the SPI for the ISAKMP Security Association.

Security Association

The Security Association field identifies the Domain of Interpretation (DOI). Since the hosts plan to run IPSec protocols between themselves, the DOI is simply IP.

Proposal Payload

Host-B's Proposal Payload will specify the protocol PROTO_ISAKMP and will set the SPI value to 0.

Transform Payload

The Transform Payload will specify KEY_OAKLEY. For the KEY_OAKLEY transform, the attributes that were accepted from the proposal offered by Host-A are copied into the appropriate fields.

At this point, the properties of the ISAKMP Security Association have been agreed to by Host-A and Host-B. The identity of the ISAKMP SA has been set equal to the pair <Cookie-A, Cookie-B>. However, the identities of the parties claiming to be Host-A and Host-B have not yet been authoritatively verified.

4.2.1.3 IKE Phase 1, Message 3

The third message of the Phase 1 ISAKMP exchange begins the exchange of the information from which the cryptographic keys will eventually be derived (see Figure 34 on page 78).

Important.

None of the messages themselves carry the actual cryptographic keys. Instead, they carry inputs that will be used by Host-A and Host-B to derive the keys locally.

The ISAKMP payload will be used to exchange two types of information:

Diffie-Hellman public value

The Diffie-Hellman public value g^x from the initiator. The exponent x in the public value is the private value that must be kept secret.

Nonce

The nonce N_i from the initiator. (*Nonce* is a fancy name for a value that is considered to be random according to some very strict mathematical guidelines.)

ID   If authentication with RSA public key is used, the nonces are encrypted with the public key of the other party. Likewise are the IDs of either party which are then also exchanged at this stage.

If authentication with revised RSA public key is used, the KE and ID payloads are encrypted with a secret key that is derived from the nonces and the encryption algorithm agreed to in Messages 1 and 2, thus avoiding one CPU-intensive public key operation.

Certificates may optionally be exchanged in either case of public key authentication, as well as a hash value thereof.

These values are carried in the Key Exchange, and the Nonce and the ID fields, respectively.

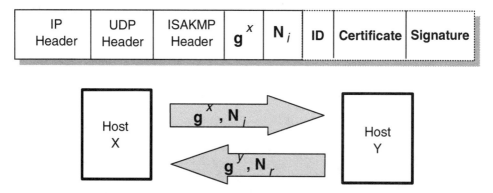

Figure 34. *Message 3 of an ISAKMP Phase 1 Exchange*

4.2.1.4 IKE Phase 1, Message 4

After receiving a Diffie-Hellman public value and a nonce from Host-A, Host-B will respond by sending to Host-A its own Diffie-Hellman public value (g^y from the responder) and its nonce (N_r from the responder).

4.2.1.5 Generating the Keys (Phase 1)

At this point, each host knows the values of the two nonces (N_i and N_r). Each host also knows its own private Diffie-Hellman value (x and y) and also knows its partner's public value (g^x or g^y). Hence each side can construct the composite value g^{xy}. And finally, each side knows the values of the initiator cookie and the responder cookie.

Given all these bits of information, each side can then independently compute identical values for the following quantities:

- SKEYID: This collection of bits is sometimes referred to as keying material, since it provides the raw input from which actual cryptographic keys will be derived later in the process. It is obtained by applying the agreed-to keyed pseudorandom function (prf) to the known inputs:

  1. For digital signature authentication:

     $$SKEYID = prf(N_i, N_r, g^{xy})$$

  2. For authentication with public keys:

```
SKEYID = prf(hash(N_i, N_r), CookieA, CookieB)
```

3. For authentication with a pre-shared key:

```
SKEYID = prf(pre-shared key, N_i, N_r)
```

- Having computed the value SKEYID, each side then proceeds to generate two cryptographic keys and some additional keying material:

    - SKEYID_d is keying material that will be subsequently used in Phase 2 to derive the keys that will be used in non-ISAKMP SAs for protecting user traffic:

    ```
    SKEYID_d = prf(SKEYID, g^{xy}, CookieA, CookieB, 0)
    ```

    - SKEYID_a is the key used for authenticating ISAKMP messages:

    ```
    SKEYID_a = prf(SKEYID, SKEYID_d, g^{xy}, CookieA, CookieB, 1)
    ```

    - SKEYID_e is the key used for encrypting ISAKMP exchanges:

    ```
    SKEYID_e = prf(SKEYID, SKEYID_a, g^{xy}, CookieA, CookieB, 2)
    ```

At this point in the protocol, both Host-A and Host-B have derived identical authentication and encryption keys that they will use to protect the ISAKMP exchanges. And they have also derived identical keying material from which they will derive keys to protect user data during Phase 2 of the ISAKMP negotiations. However, at this point, the two parties' identities still have not been authenticated to one another.

4.2.1.6 IKE Phase 1, Message 5

At this point in the Phase 1 flows, the two hosts will exchange identity information with each other to authenticate themselves. As shown in Figure 35 on page 80, the ISAKMP message will carry an identity payload, a signature payload, and an optional certificate payload. Host-A uses Message 5 to send information to Host-B that will allow Host-B to authenticate Host-A.

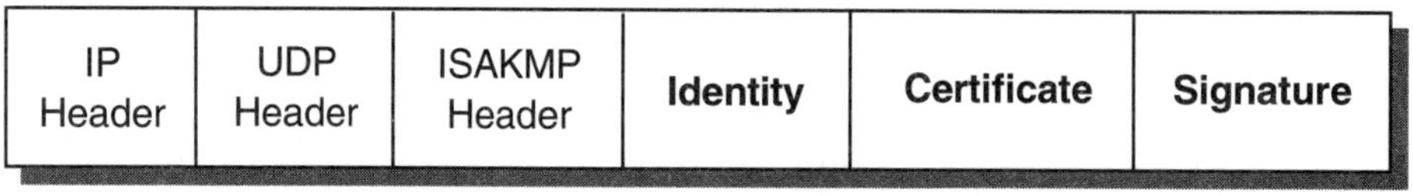

IP Header	UDP Header	ISAKMP Header	**Identity**	**Certificate**	**Signature**

Figure 35. Message 5 of an ISAKMP Phase 1 Exchange

When an actual certificate is present in the Certificate Payload field, the receiver can use the information directly, after verifying that it has been signed with a valid signature of a trusted certificate authority. If there is no certificate in the message, then it is the responsibility of the receiver to obtain a certificate using some implementation method. For example, it may send a query to a trusted certificate authority using a protocol such as LDAP, or it may query a secure DNS server, or it may maintain a secure local cache that maps previously used certificates to their respective ID values, or it may send an ISAKMP Certificate Request message to its peer, who must then immediately send its certificate to the requester.

Note: The method for obtaining a certificate is a local option, and is not defined as part of IKE. In particular, it is a local responsibility of the receiver to check that the certificate in question is still valid and has not been revoked.

There are several points to bear in mind:

- At this stage of the process, all ISAKMP payloads, whether in Phase 1 or Phase 2, are encrypted, using the encryption algorithm (negotiated in Messages 1 and 2) and the keys (derived from the information in Messages 3 and 4). The ISAKMP header itself, however, is still transmitted in the clear.

- In Phase 1, IPSec's ESP protocol is not used: that is, there is no ESP header. The recipient uses the Encryption Bit in the Flags field of the ISAKMP header to determine if encryption has been applied to the message. The pair of values <CookieA, CookieB>, which serve as an SPI for Phase 1 exchanges, provide a pointer to the correct algorithm and key to be used to decrypt the message.

- The Digital Signature, if used, is not applied to the ISAKMP message itself. Instead, it is applied to a hash of information that is available to both Host-A and Host-B.

- The identity carried in the identity payload does not necessarily bear any relationship to the source IP address; however, the identity carried in the identity payload must be the identity to which the certificate, if used, applies.

Host-A (the initiator) will generate the following hash function, and then place the result in the Signature Payload field:

```
HASH_I = prf(SKEYID, gˣ, gʸ, CookieA, CookieB, SAₚ, ID_A)
```

If digital signatures were used for authentication, this hash will also be signed by Host-A.

ID_A is Host-A's identity information that was transmitted in the identity payload of this message, and SA_p is the entire body of the SA payload that was sent by Host-A in Message 1, including all proposals and all transforms proposed by Host-A. The cookies, public Diffie-Hellman values, and SKEYID were explicitly carried in Messages 1 through 4, or were derived from their contents.

4.2.1.7 IKE Phase 1, Message 6

After receiving Message 5 from Host-A, Host-B will verify the identity of Host-A by validating the hash.

If digital signatures were used for authentication, the signature of this hash will be verified by Host-B.

If this is successful, then Host-B will send Message 6 to Host-A to allow Host-A to verify the identity of Host-B.

The structure of Message 6 is the same as that of Message 5, with the obvious changes that the identity payload and the certificate payload now pertain to Host-B.

```
HASH_R = prf(SKEYID, gʸ, gˣ, CookieB, CookieA, SAₚ, ID_B)
```

Notice that the order in which Diffie-Hellman public values and the cookies appear has been changed, and the final term now is the Identity Payload that Host-B has included in Message 6.

If digital signatures were used for authentication, this hash will also be signed by Host-B, which is different from the one previously signed by Host-A.

When Host-A receives Message 6 and verifies the hash or digital signature, the Phase 1 exchanges are then complete. At this point, each participant has authenticated itself to its peer. Both have agreed on the characteristics of the ISAKMP Security Associations, and both have derived the same set of keys (or keying material).

4.2.1.8 Miscellaneous Phase 1 Facts

There are several miscellaneous facts worth noting:

1. Regardless of the specific authentication mechanism that is used, there will be six messages exchanged for Oakley Main Mode. However, the content of the individual messages will differ, depending on the authentication method.
2. Although Oakley exchanges make use of both encryption and authentication, they do not use either IPSec's ESP or AH protocol. ISAKMP exchanges are protected with application-layer security mechanisms, not with network layer security mechanisms.
3. ISAKMP messages are sent using UDP. There is no guaranteed delivery for them.
4. The only way to identify that an ISAKMP message is part of a Phase 1 flow rather than a Phase 2 flow is to check the Message ID field in the ISAKMP Header. For Phase 1 flows, it must be 0, and (although not explicitly stated in the ISAKMP documents) for Phase 2 flows it must be non-zero.

4.2.2 Phase 2 - Setting Up the Protocol Security Associations

After having completed the Phase 1 negotiation process to set up the ISAKMP Security Associations, Host-A's next step is to initiate the Oakley Phase 2 message exchanges (also known as Oakley Quick Mode) to define the security associations and keys that will be used to protect IP datagrams exchanged between the pair of users. (In the Internet Drafts, these are referred to somewhat obtusely as "non-ISAKMP SAs".)

Because the purpose of the Phase 1 negotiations was to agree on how to protect ISAKMP messages, all ISAKMP Phase 2 payloads, but not the ISAKMP header itself, must be encrypted using the algorithm agreed to by the Phase 1 negotiations.

When Oakley Quick Mode is used in Phase 2, authentication is achieved via the use of several cryptographically based hash functions. The input to the hash functions comes partly from Phase 1 information (SKEYID) and partly from information exchanged in Phase 2. Phase 2 authentication is based on certificates, but the Phase 2 process itself does not use certificates directly. Instead, it uses the SKEYID_a material from Phase 1, which itself was authenticated via certificates.

Oakley Quick Mode comes in two forms:

- Without a Key Exchange attribute, Quick Mode can be used to refresh the cryptographic keys, but does not provide the property of Perfect Forward Secrecy (PFS).

- With a Key Exchange attribute, Quick Mode can be used to refresh the cryptographic keys in a way that provides PFS. This is accomplished by including an exchange of public Diffie-Hellman values within messages 1 and 2.

Note: PFS apparently is a property that is very much desired by cryptography experts, but strangely enough, the specs treat PFS as optional. They mandate that a system must be capable of handling the Key Exchange field when it is present in a Quick Mode message, but do not require a system to include the field within the message.

The detailed description of the Phase 2 messages and exchanged information follows below:

4.2.2.1 IKE Phase 2, Message 1

Message 1 of a Quick Mode Exchange allows Host-A to authenticate itself, to select a nonce, to propose security association(s) to Host-B, to execute an exchange of public Diffie-Hellman values, and to indicate if it is acting on its own behalf or as a proxy negotiator for another entity. An overview of the format of Message 1 is shown in Figure 36.

Note: Inclusion of a key exchange field is optional. However, when Perfect Forward Secrecy is desired, it must be present.

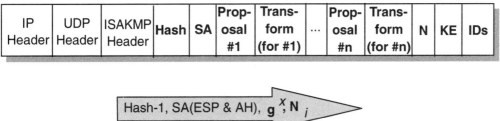

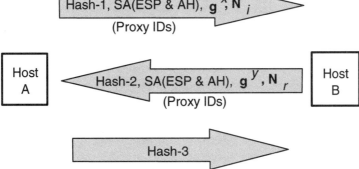

Figure 36. Message 1 of an ISAKMP Phase 2 Quick Mode Exchange

Since we have assumed that Host-A and Host-B are each acting on their own behalf, the user identity fields illustrated in Figure 36 will not be present. The message will consist of:

ISAKMP Header

The ISAKMP Header will indicate an exchange type of Quick Mode, will include a non-zero Message-ID chosen by Host-A, will include the initiator and responder cookie values chosen in Phase 1 (that is, Cookie-A and Cookie-B), and will turn on the encryption flag to indicate that the payloads of the ISAKMP message are encrypted according to the algorithm and key negotiated during Phase 1.

Hash

A Hash Payload must immediately follow the ISAKMP header. HASH_1 uses the keyed pseudo-random function that was negotiated during the Phase 1 exchanges, and is derived from the following information:

- SKEYID_a was derived from the Phase 1 exchanges.
- M-ID is the message ID of this message.
- SA is the Security Association payload carried in this message, including all proposals that were offered.
- Nonce is a new value different from the one used in Phase 1.
- KE is the public Diffie-Hellman value carried in this message. This quantity is chosen by Host-A, and is denoted as g_{qm}^x. Note that this is not the same quantity as g^x that was used in the Phase 1 exchanges.
- IDs, which can identify either the endpoints of the Phase 1 exchange or endpoints on whose behalf the protocol SA should be negotiated (proxy IDs when IKE is used in client mode). These can subsequently be different from the IDs used in Phase 1.

Note: The use of KE and ID is optional depending if PFS is desired.

$$\text{HASH\_1} = \text{prf}(\text{SKEYID\_a, M-ID, SA, } N_{qmi}, \text{ KE, } ID_{qmi}, ID_{qmr})$$

Security Association

Indicate IP as the Domain of Interpretation.

Proposal, Transform Pairs

There can be one or more of these pairs in this message. The first proposal payload will be numbered 1, will identify an IPSec protocol to be used, and will include an SPI value that is randomly chosen by Host-A for use with that protocol. The proposal payload will be followed by a single transform payload that indicates the cryptographic algorithm to be used with that protocol. The second proposal payload will be numbered 2, etc.

Nonce Payload

This contains the nonce N^{qmi} that was chosen randomly by Host-A.

KE This is the key exchange payload that will carry the public Diffie-Hellman value chosen by Host-A, $g_{qm}{}^x$. There is also a field called Group, that indicates the prime number and generator used in the Diffie-Hellman exchange.

ID Payload

Specifies the endpoints for this SA.

4.2.2.2 IKE Phase 2, Message 2

After Host-B receives Message 1 from Host-A and successfully authenticates it using HASH_1, it constructs a reply, Message 2, to be sent back to Host-A. The Message ID of the reply will be the same one that Host-A used in Message 1. Host-B will choose new values for the following:

Hash

The hash payload now carries the value HASH_2, which is defined as:

$$\text{HASH\_2} = \text{prf}(\text{SKEYID\_a}, N_{qmi}, \text{M-ID}, \text{SA}, N_{qmr}, \text{KE}, ID_{qmi}, ID_{qmr})$$

Security Association

The Security Association payload only describes the single chosen proposal and its associated transforms, not all of the protection suites offered by Host-A. Host-B also chooses an SPI value for the selected protocol. Host-B's SPI does not depend in any way on the SPI that Host-A assigned to that protocol when it offered the proposal. That is, it is not necessary that SPI_A be the same as SPI_B; it is only necessary that they each be non-zero and that they each be randomly chosen.

Nonce

Nonce payload now carries N_r, a random value chosen by Host-B.

KE Key exchange payload now carries Host-B's public Diffie-Hellman value, $g_{qm}{}^y$.

At this point, Host-A and Host-B have exchanged nonces and public Diffie-Hellman values. Each one can use this in conjunction with other information to derive a pair of keys, one for each direction of transmission.

4.2.2.3 Generating the Keys (Phase 2)

Using the nonces, public Diffie-Hellman values, SPIs, protocol code points exchanged in Messages 1 and 2 of Phase 2, and the SKEYID value from Phase 1, each host now has enough information to derive two sets of keying material.

1. When PFS is used:

   - For data generated by Host-A and received by Host-B, the keying material is:

   $$\text{KEYMAT}_{AB} = \text{prf}(\text{SKEYID\_d}, g_{qm}{}^{xy}, \text{protocol}, \text{SPI}_B, N_{qmi}, N_{qmr})$$

   - For data generated by Host-B and received by Host-A, the keying material is:

   $$\text{KEYMAT}_{BA} = \text{prf}(\text{SKEYID\_d}, g_{qm}{}^{xy}, \text{protocol}, \text{SPI}_A, N_{qmi}, N_{qmr})$$

2. When PFS is not used:

   - For data generated by Host-A and received by Host-B, the keying material is:

   $$\text{KEYMAT}_{AB} = \text{prf}(\text{SKEYID\_d}, \text{protocol}, \text{SPI}_B, N_{qmi}, N_{qmr})$$

   - For data generated by Host-B and received by Host-A, the keying material is:

   $$\text{KEYMAT}_{BA} = \text{prf}(\text{SKEYID\_d}, \text{protocol}, \text{SPI}_A, N_{qmi}, N_{qmr})$$

Note: Depending on the particular case, Host-A may need to derive multiple keys for the following purposes:

- Generating the integrity check value for transmitted datagrams
- Validating the integrity check value of received datagrams
- Encrypting transmitted datagrams
- Decrypting received datagrams

Likewise, Host-B needs to derive the mirror image of the same keys. For example, the key that Host-B uses to encrypt its outbound messages is the same key that Host-A uses to decrypt its inbound messages, etc.

4.2.2.4 IKE Phase 2, Message 3

At this point, Host-A and Host-B have exchanged all the information necessary for them to derive the necessary keying material. The third message in the Quick Mode exchange is used by Host-A to prove its liveness, which it does by producing a hash function that covers the message ID and both nonces that were exchanged in Messages 1 and 2. Message 3 consists only of the ISAKMP header and a hash payload that carries:

```
HASH_3 = prf(SKEYID_a, 0, M-ID, N_qmi, N_qmr)
```

When Host-B receives this message and verifies the hash, then both systems can begin
to use the negotiated security protocols to protect their user data streams.

4.3 Negotiating Multiple Security Associations

As explained earlier, a non-ISAKMP security association is negotiated by means of a
Quick Mode message exchange. However, it is also possible to negotiate multiple
security associations, each with its own set of keying material, within a single
3-message Quick Mode exchange.

The message formats are very similar to the previously illustrated ones, so only the
differences will be highlighted below:

- Message 1 will carry multiple security association payloads, each offering a range
  of protection suites.

- HASH_1 will cover the entire set of all offered Security Associations carried in
  Message 1. That is, each Security Association and all of its offered proposals are
  included.

- In Message 2, for each offered SA, Host-B will select a single protection suite.
  That is, if n SAs are open for negotiation, then Host-B will choose n protection
  suites, one from each proposal.

- As was the case for HASH_1, HASH_2 will now cover the entire set of all
  offered security associations carried in Message 1. That is, each security
  association and all of its offered proposals are included.

- After Messages 1 and 2 have been exchanged, then Host-A and Host-B will be
  able to generate the keying material for each of the accepted protection suites,
  using the same formulas as in 4.2.2.3, "Generating the Keys (Phase 2)" on
  page 85, applied individually for each accepted SA. Even though the nonces and
  the public Diffie-Hellman values are the same for all selected suites, the keying
  material derived for each selected protection suite will be different because each
  proposal will have a different SPI.

- Because multiple security associations have been negotiated, it is a matter of local
  choice as to which one is used to protect a given datagram. A receiving system
  must be capable of processing a datagram that is protected by any SA that has
  been negotiated. That is, it would be legal for a given source host to send two

consecutive datagrams to a destination system, where each datagram was protected by a different SA.

4.4 Using ISAKMP/Oakley with Remote Access

The critical element in the remote access scenario is the use of ISAKMP/Oakley to identify the remote host by name, rather than by its dynamically assigned IP address. Once the remote host's identity has been authenticated and the mapping to its dynamically assigned IP address has been ascertained, the remainder of the processes are the same as we have described for the other scenarios. For example, if the corporate intranet is considered to be trusted, then the remote host needs to establish a single SA between itself and the firewall. But if the corporate intranet is considered to be untrusted, then it may be necessary for the remote host to set up two SAs: one between itself and the firewall, and a second between itself and the destination host.

Recall that a single ISAKMP Phase 1 negotiation can protect several subsequent Phase 2 negotiations. Phase 1 ISAKMP negotiations use computationally intensive public key cryptographic operations, while Phase 2 negotiations use the less computationally intensive symmetric key cryptographic operations. Hence, the heavy computational load only occurs in Phase I, which will only be executed once when the dial-up connection is first initiated.

The principal points that pertain to the remote access case are:

- The remote host's dynamically assigned address is the one that is placed in the IP header of all ISAKMP messages.

- The remote host's permanent identifier (such as an e-mail address) is the quantity that is placed in the ID field of the ISAKMP Phase 1 messages.

- The remote host's certificate used in the ISAKMP exchange must be associated with the remote host's permanent identifier.

- In traffic-bearing datagrams, the remote host's dynamically assigned IP address will be used. This is necessary since the destination IP address that appears in the datagram's IP header is used in conjunction with the SPI and protocol type to identify the relevant IPSec security association for processing the inbound datagram.

Chapter 5. Branch Office Connection Scenario

This chapter shows the most common use of VPN technology, the secure connection of two trusted intranets over the public Internet. The focus in this scenario is on protecting your intranets from outside attacks and securing corporate data flowing on the Internet.

This scenario can be also deployed in one intranet. It may be reasonable to connect in this way, for example, two highly secure development laboratory networks over the existing corporate network infrastructure.

Consider a company that was running its own private network, using its own routers, bridges, and private lines. If the company had campuses at geographically dispersed sites, it may prove more economical to break the corporate network into pieces (the intranets), add a firewall to control traffic flow across the intranet/Internet boundary, and then procure service from one or more ISPs to interconnect the intranets over the Internet backbone.

For this example, we assume that company A just wants to enable communication between its intranets, but does not necessarily want to communicate with entities outside of company A.

5.1 Design Considerations

Let us consider how company A could construct a virtual private network for interconnecting its intranets securely. In the discussion we do not take into account the basic Internet access issues, since these can be well separated and are outside the scope of this redbook.

5.1.1 Authenticating Backbone Traffic

The Internet will be carrying traffic not just from company A's VPN, but also from other VPNs. Company A's firewalls must admit only traffic from company A's VPNs and must reject all other incoming traffic. They might admit non-VPN incoming traffic destined to them in case they provide general Internet connectivity, for example, if they operate proxies or SOCKS servers. However, in the case of a large company with many VPNs it is worth considering the separation of functions, that is, dedicated security gateways for VPNs and others for general Internet access. It is more expensive but dedicated VPN gateways are much harder to bring down by denial of service attacks, because they accept only authenticated traffic. Companies in most cases are much more sensible to the loss of branch connectivity than to the loss of Web access.

Deploying IPSec's authentication protocols in company A's firewalls (or IPSec-enabled routers) at the intranet boundary will accomplish these goals. IPSec's authentication techniques are cryptographically strong, so they provide significantly better protection against address spoofing and denial of service attacks than would rely on conventional, non-cryptographic filtering techniques. In this scenario, cryptographic authentication using HMAC will be the first line of defense. Having established that the traffic has come from somewhere within company A's network, non-cryptographic filtering can then be used as the second line of defense to provide more granular access control, if desired.

5.1.2 Data Confidentiality

It should be obvious that company A will want to keep its data confidential (that is, encrypted) while it is in transit across the public Internet. But it is not always clear if the data should also be protected when it flows within its own intranets. If the company had not previously encrypted its internal traffic when it used a monolithic private network, it may not see value in encrypting it when it flows within its intranets.

If a company does not believe that it is subject to internally mounted attacks, the simplest solution will be to encrypt and authenticate traffic flowing between firewalls, and make no security-related changes to the end systems themselves. This has the advantage of much fewer security associations to manage: two per firewall for bidirectional data flow, compared to two per host for host-to-host encryption. But it has the disadvantage that traffic is exposed to relatively simple attacks while it flows in the intranet. Since authentication is also needed between firewalls, the simplest branch office VPN will use ESP in tunnel mode with authentication between the two firewalls. Another solution is the combination of AH and ESP in tunnel mode, which has the advantage of authentication of the outer IP header as well, thus avoiding the denial of service attacks. The latter is the only possibility to provide both authentication and encryption when the firewall product does not yet support the latest IPSec specifications.

This is the situation described in the 3.4.2, "Case 2: Basic VPN Support" on page 64 in Chapter 3, "Description of IPSec" on page 47.

For considerations on how to configure a VPN solution between branch offices that can protect you against threats both in the Internet and in your company's intranet as well, please refer to Chapter 6, "Business Partner/Supplier Network Scenario" on page 103 where we discuss this topic in the slightly different context of two different companies. However, the solution is the same.

5.1.3 Addressing Issues

We assumed that company A previously had a traditional network in place, where its various intranets were interconnected over private facilities, such as leased lines or frame relay. We also assumed that company A has already developed an address plan for its network. Since the network was self-contained and the backbone used only private facilities, company A could have used either globally ambiguous (private) IP addresses (that is, of the form 10.x.y.z) or globally unique (public) addresses obtained from the Network Information Center (NIC).

Because assignment of public IP addresses is coordinated through a global authority, they are unambiguous. Public addresses are routable everywhere. However, because private address assignments are facilitated locally without coordination by a global authority, they are ambiguous when used in the public Internet; they are routable only within a company's own private network.

In summary:

1. If company A uses public addresses in its network, the addresses can continue to be used without change in the VPN environment. If it is desired to hide them while the datagram is in transit over the Internet, an ESP tunnel can be used between firewalls.
2. If company A uses private IP addresses in its network, the addresses can also continue to be used on all subnets that have no physical connection to the public Internet. But for those subnets that do connect to the public Internet, typically the exit links at the boundary of the intranet, a public IP address must be used.

ESP tunnel mode or AH and ESP in tunnel mode between firewalls handles both situations. The tunnel's new IP header will use the global addresses of the two firewalls, allowing datagrams to be routed over the Internet between the two firewalls (or routers). The header of the original (inner) IP datagram will use the IP addresses assigned for use in the intranet; since these addresses will be hidden from view by ESP's encryption protocol, they can be either publicly or privately assigned.

5.1.4 Routing Issues

Because a VPN in fact resembles a set of IP networks, all but the smallest VPNs will typically need to deploy an IP routing protocol between the gateway machines (firewalls or routers) at the boundaries of the company's intranets. Routing protocols typically exchange information that will describe the topology of the VPN. That is, the topology updates will describe the IP addresses that are reachable within each intranet that participates in the VPN. IPSec can be used to both encrypt and authenticate the routing information, thus hiding topological details of the intranet as they are exchanged across the public network.

The company's network administrator(s) can incorporate conventional IP routing protocols into the firewalls, and then use IPSec protocols to encrypt and authenticate the exchange of routing information among the firewalls. Figure 37 illustrates this concept schematically for a sample configuration that consists of three branch offices of a given company that need to communicate among themselves via the public Internet.

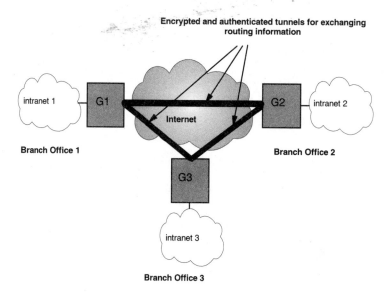

Figure 37. Exchanging Routing Information Securely

When an IPSec tunnel is established between a pair of firewalls, they appear to be logically adjacent to one another, even though there may be several routers along the actual physical path. Each pair of virtually adjacent security gateways will set up a security association between themselves, using ESP in tunnel mode with authentication or AH and ESP in tunnel mode to provide both encryption and authentication. The routing information that is exchanged will then be hidden from view because it will have been encrypted.

Because the set of firewalls participate in a common routing protocol, they will know the correct firewall for reaching any given destination host within the intranets. Hence, traffic arriving at an exit firewall can be sent via an ESP tunnel, using its authentication option or a combined AH-ESP tunnel, and can then be authenticated by the entry firewall that protects the remote branch office's Intranet.

Thus, IPSec makes it possible to exchange routing information and user data between branch offices over the Internet while preserving the confidentiality of both user data and intranet topology information. Because routing information (for example, IP addresses) is visible only to other members of the corporate network, this scheme can be used regardless of whether addresses used in the interior of an intranet are globally unique or privately assigned.

To be more specific, since the intranet addresses are carried within encrypted routing update messages, they are neither visible to, nor used by, any of the routers in the Internet. Therefore, if company A's intranets use a self-consistent addressing scheme, either public or private, network address translation is not needed for intranet addresses. Encapsulating encryption already hides the interior addresses, and all backbone routing is based only on the public IP addresses of the boundary gateways. Finally, depending on the sophistication of the routing algorithms, it may also be possible to support redundant entry/exit points into a corporate network.

5.1.5 Summary: Branch Office Connection

This application replaces existing private lines or leased lines in a corporate network, and uses the public Internet as the backbone for interconnecting a company's branch offices. (This solution is not limited only to branch offices, but can also be be applied between any collection of a company's geographically dispersed sites, such as labs, manufacturing plants, warehouses, etc.) This solution does not mandate any changes in the clients (PCs or servers) unless it is desired to protect against internal attacks as well as external ones.

The design features are:

- Client machines (hosts and servers) need not support IPSec if the intranets are considered to be trusted and secure. This minimizes the migration issues of moving to a VPN approach and maintains the pre-existing host-to-host security policies and procedures of the original network. IPSec support will be required only at the intranet boundaries, that is, in the VPN gateway boxes. Also there will be no security-related protocols required in any of the routers, bridges, or switches that are located either in the interior of the intranets or in the public backbone Internet.

- VPN gateways situated at the perimeter of each branch office intranet implement the basic firewall functions (for example, packet filtering) and also support IPSec protocols to build secure and authenticated tunnels between all VPN gateways of the branch office networks that comprise the VPN.

User data traffic will be both authenticated and encrypted. Any inbound traffic that can not be authenticated by the VPN gateway will not be delivered into the intranet. Authentication will be cryptographically based, using AH or the authentication option for IPSec's ESP protocol.

- Routing control messages will be exchanged among the set of VPN gateways, and these messages will also be encrypted and authenticated using IPSec procedures.

- If the number of VPN gateways in the initial VPN deployment is small, key distribution and security association definition can be handled by manual methods. But as the VPN's size grows to encompass more and more intranets, the automated IBM tunnel (see A.1.2, "Tunnel Types" on page 121) or ISAKMP/Oakley procedures will rapidly become a necessity.

- Security associations will be set up among the set of VPN gateways. Because the source and destination hosts (that is, clients and servers) are not required to support IPSec, no security associations need to be set up between hosts, and no keys need to be assigned to them. In the future, if even stronger security is desired for host-to-host communications, then clients and servers will need to support the IPSec protocols.

- The IP addresses assigned for use in the intranets can be used as is, regardless of whether they were assigned from a public or a private address space. Only the interfaces of the VPN gateways that attach to the Internet backbone are required to use globally unique IP addresses.

- Packet filtering rules, if any, that were used in the pre-VPN network should be installed on the VPN gateway to control traffic that enters the branch office intranet. They can be used as a second line of defense, after the packets have been authenticated by IPSec's AH protocol.

- If end-to-end IPSec functions are deployed between hosts, then new packet filtering rules will be needed in the firewalls to recognize the IPSec AH and ESP headers.

5.2 How Does It Work?

This section follows the packet on the way from one endpoint to the other in order to understand the filter rules necessary for the connection. But before we follow the way a packet travels let us first list the filter rules used for the branch office scenario.

5.2.1 Filter Rules for Tunnel Traffic

For better reading we took out the IP addresses and network masks and replaced them with:

FW1: IP address of firewall 1

FW2: IP address of firewall 2

SN1: Secure network of firewall 1

SN2: Secure network of firewall 2

NM: Network mask of the object

- Firewalls: 255.255.255.255

- Networks: 255.255.255.0 (in our case)

We have also replaced the real tunnel ID with x and numbered the rules (in parentheses, at the end of each rule) so that we can reference them later on throughout the explanations. The two connections (four services) of our configuration example produced the following rules on FW1:

```
#        Between both firewalls
#          Service : VPN encapsulation
# Description : Permit encrypted data between firewalls
permit FW1 NM FW2 NM ah any 0 any 0 non-secure local both l=y f=y       (1)
permit FW2 NM FW1 NM ah any 0 any 0 non-secure local both l=y f=y       (2)
permit FW1 NM FW2 NM esp any 0 any 0 non-secure local both l=y f=y      (3)
permit FW2 NM FW1 NM esp any 0 any 0 non-secure local both l=y f=y      (4)


#        Between both firewalls
#          Service : VPN key exchange
# Description : Permit session key exchanges for IBM tunnels
permit FW1 NM FW2 NM udp eq 4001 eq 4001 non-secure local both l=y f=y  (5)
permit FW2 NM FW1 NM udp eq 4001 eq 4001 non-secure local both l=y f=y  (6)


#        Between both secure networks
#          Service : VPN traffic 1/2
# Description : Permit routed traffic on secure interface (non-encrypted)
permit SN1 NM SN2 NM all any 0 any 0 secure route inbound l=y f=y       (7)
permit SN2 NM SN1 NM all any 0 any 0 secure route outbound l=y f=y      (8)


#        Between both secure networks
#          Service : VPN traffic 2/2 (tunnel x)
# Description : Permit routed traffic on non-secure interface (encrypted)
permit SN1 NM SN2 NM all any 0 any 0 non-secure route outbound l=y f=y t=x (9)
permit SN2 NM SN1 NM all any 0 any 0 non-secure route inbound l=y f=y t=x (10)
```

Figure 38. Tunnel Filter Rules on FW1

Note: Actually the standard description of the last service above is not precise. This service sends traffic to the the IPSec kernel for encryption (and receives it from there), but when passing the rules of this service the packet is in the clear (non-encrypted).

The above filter rules allow for tunnel traffic between any hosts in both secure networks. The following section explains the journey of a packet from Host H1 to Host H2 through a tunnel between FW1 and FW2 (as shown in Figure 39).

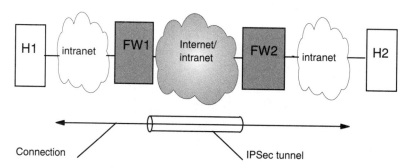

Figure 39. Tunnel between Firewalls FW1 And FW2, Traffic between Hosts H1 And H2

5.2.2 The Flow of a Packet

Now let us take a journey from one tunnel endpoint to the other. We start our travel at the originating host H1 located in the secure network of FW1 and get to the secure network interface of FW1 via our intranet. That's where Figure 40 starts on the left-hand side.

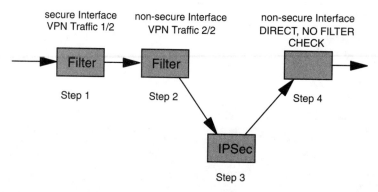

Figure 40. Outbound Packet Flow on Firewall FW1

The figure shows the way of the packet from entering the firewall on the secure interface until it leaves the firewall on its way to the Internet. Let's discuss the details:

Note: The original packet header carries H1 as source address and H2 as destination address. The message starts in the clear.

Step 1

> The packet is allowed by rule 7 of Figure 38 on page 95. Because ipforwarding is enabled, the firewall forwards the packet to the non-secure interface of FW1.

Step 2

> During the check of the filter rules for the non-secure interface, the definitions of rule 9 are matched. Because this rule defines a non-zero tunnel ID, the packet is sent to the IPSec kernel for processing instead of being sent out to the Internet.

Step 3

> The IPSec kernel examines the tunnel ID and processes the packet according to the definitions of the corresponding security association (SA). Our SA defines tunnel mode and the policy encr/auth. Therefore the packet is first encrypted, then authenticated and also gets a new IP header (tunnel mode) with source and destination IP addresses of the firewalls FW1 and FW2.

Step 4

> The IPSec kernel will *not* send the packet through the filters again. For performance reasons the packet is instead sent straight through the non-secure interface to the Internet.

The packet then passes the remote firewall FW2 on the way to its final destination host H2. Let us explore the return path on FW1 again (which also explains what happened on FW2).

Figure 41 on page 98 shows the way of the packet from arrival at the non-secure interface of the firewall until leaving the firewall through the secure interface on its way back to host H1.

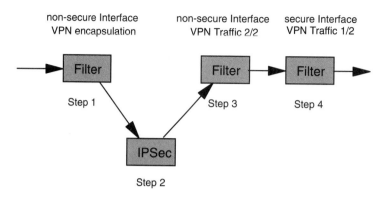

non-secure Interface   non-secure Interface   secure Interface
VPN encapsulation   VPN Traffic 2/2   VPN Traffic 1/2

Figure 41. Inbound Packet Flow on Firewall FW1 (marco)

Step 1

The packet gets checked by the filter rule base and matches rule 2 of Figure 38 on page 95 (in our case, because AH was the last protocol applied). Because it carries an IPSec header, the packet will be sent to the IPSec kernel. Up to now the packet is authenticated and encrypted.

Step 2

The IPSec kernel examines the tunnel ID and processes the packet according to the definitions of the corresponding security association(s) (SA). In our case the packet is first authenticated and then decrypted, which means that authentication takes place according to the SPI indicated in the AH header. That header is then stripped off, exposing the ESP header to which the former AH header's next header field is pointing. Decryption is performed accoring to the SPI indicated in the ESP header, which is then stripped of, exposing the original datagram's IP header. For better understanding of this process, the whole IP datagram as it is received by the IPSec kernel is shown in Figure 42:

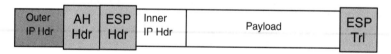

| Outer IP Hdr | AH Hdr | ESP Hdr | Inner IP Hdr | Payload | ESP Trl |

Figure 42. IP Packet Inside a Combined AH-ESP Tunnel

The additional tunnel mode IP header (containing the two firewall addresses) is also removed.

Now the source IP address host H2 and destination IP address host H1 are in the outermost IP header again. The IPSec kernel sends the packet again to the non-secure interface.

Note: If the authentication of the packet fails, it is discarded by the IPSec kernel right away. In that case the firewall logs a message (invalid IPSec package) that you can scan for to find out if someone tries to mount a denial-of-service attack.

Step 3

The packet is checked by the filter rule base and matches rule 10. Routing is enabled; therefore the packet is forwarded to the secure interface.

Step 4

On this interface the packet matches rule 8 and is sent to the intranet where it finally arrives back at host H1.

The additional rules 5 and 6 (udp 4001) are necessary to enable the automatic key refresh between IBM firewalls. They are not needed if you use manual or dynamic tunnels. The default rules allow AH and ESP packets between the firewalls. Actually in our case we could as well delete rules 3 and 4. We use ESP, but it is encapsulated within AH; therefore on the Internet (and also in every trace) there will be only AH packets.

5.3 Variations of the Branch Office Scenario

Up to now we have discussed the basic branch office scenario. It may vary in different ways. Below we picked out three cases.

5.3.1 Allow Only Firewall-to-Firewall Traffic

Sometimes it may be desirable to create a tunnel between two firewalls and permit only traffic between the firewalls themselves (for instance, if you would like to be able to administer one firewall from another remote firewall).

The tunnel definition will be the same as described above, but you will have to change the packet filters as shown below:

```
#        Between both firewalls
#          Service : VPN encapsulation
# Description : Permit encrypted data between firewalls
permit FW1 NM FW2 NM ah any 0 any 0 non-secure local both l=y f=y        (1)
permit FW2 NM FW1 NM ah any 0 any 0 non-secure local both l=y f=y        (2)
permit FW1 NM FW2 NM esp any 0 any 0 non-secure local both l=y f=y       (3)
permit FW2 NM FW1 NM esp any 0 any 0 non-secure local both l=y f=y       (4)


#        Between both firewalls
#          Service : VPN key exchange
# Description : Permit session key exchanges for IBM tunnels
permit FW1 NM FW2 NM udp eq 4001 eq 4001 non-secure local both l=y f=y   (5)
permit FW2 NM FW1 NM udp eq 4001 eq 4001 non-secure local both l=y f=y   (6)


#        Between both firewalls
#          Service : VPN traffic (tunnel x)
# Description : Permit local traffic on non-secure interface (encrypted)
permit FW1 NM FW2 NM all any 0 any 0 non-secure local outbound l=y f=y t=x (7)
permit FW2 NM FW1 NM all any 0 any 0 non-secure local inbound l=y f=y t=x  (8)
```

Figure 43. Filter Rules for Firewall-to-Firewall Traffic

This will allow any traffic between both firewalls through tunnel x. Rules 1 to 6 stayed the same; we only modified rules 7 and 8. We do not need rules 9 and 10 anymore, because the firewall tunnel traffic takes only place at the non-secure interface. Apart from the packet filter change above the whole firewall setup stays the same. Because the tunnel traffic is restricted to both firewalls, you are now able to put all tunnel related filter rules into one connection (source object FW1, destination object FW2). Don't forget that those definitions are required on both firewalls.

5.3.2 Allow Only Certain Kinds of Traffic

Within the base branch office scenario there are no restrictions concerning the type of traffic flowing through the tunnel. You may wish to restrict the traffic between the two secure networks to certain activities. You only need to change the connection handling the tunnel traffic between the two secure networks on both firewalls in order to accomplish restrictions. In the example below we restricted the tunnel traffic to the TCP protocol. Everything else (such as ICMP, UDP and so on) is rejected. The other tunnel filter rules (1-6) stay the same.

```
#       Between both firewalls
#           Service : VPN encapsulation
# Description : Permit encrypted data between firewalls
permit FW1 NM FW2 NM ah any 0 any 0 non-secure local both l=y f=y      (1)
permit FW2 NM FW1 NM ah any 0 any 0 non-secure local both l=y f=y      (2)
permit FW1 NM FW2 NM esp any 0 any 0 non-secure local both l=y f=y     (3)
permit FW2 NM FW1 NM esp any 0 any 0 non-secure local both l=y f=y     (4)


#       Between both firewalls
#           Service : VPN key exchange
# Description : Permit session key exchanges for IBM tunnels
permit FW1 NM FW2 NM udp eq 4001 eq 4001 non-secure local both l=y f=y  (5)
permit FW2 NM FW1 NM udp eq 4001 eq 4001 non-secure local both l=y f=y  (6)


#       Between both secure networks
#           Service : VPN traffic 1/2
# Description : Permit routed traffic on secure interface (non-encrypted)
permit SN1 NM SN2 NM tcp any 0 any 0 secure route inbound l=y f=y      (7)
permit SN2 NM SN1 NM tcp any 0 any 0 secure route outbound l=y f=y     (8)


#           Service : VPN traffic 2/2 (tunnel x)
# Description : Permit routed traffic on non-secure interface (encrypted)
permit SN1 NM SN2 NM tcp any 0 any 0 non-secure route outbound l=y f=y t=x (9)
permit SN2 NM SN1 NM tcp any 0 any 0 non-secure route inbound l=y f=y t=x (10)
```

Figure 44. Filter Rules for Special Traffic

5.3.3 Allow Only Traffic between Specific Hosts

Another variation of the branch office scenario is that you still trust your secure
networks but you only want to allow specific hosts to use the tunnel to connect to the
remote secure network.

The only difference to the base setup described is again in the filter rule base. For the
connection between the secure networks (rules 7 to 10 in 5.2, "How Does It Work?"
on page 94) you have to exchange the network objects to the hosts you want to grant
tunnel usage. Of course it is possible to put multiple hosts into network object groups
and use the group objects instead. The example below assumes that you only want to
allow the hosts H1 and H2 access through the tunnel. For this example we assume
that you have created two network objects called H1 and H2. Remember the changes
need to be done on both firewalls.

```
#       Between both firewalls
#         Service : VPN encapsulation
# Description : Permit encrypted data between firewalls
permit FW1 NM FW2 NM ah any 0 any 0 non-secure local both l=y f=y      (1)
permit FW2 NM FW1 NM ah any 0 any 0 non-secure local both l=y f=y      (2)
permit FW1 NM FW2 NM esp any 0 any 0 non-secure local both l=y f=y     (3)
permit FW2 NM FW1 NM esp any 0 any 0 non-secure local both l=y f=y     (4)


#       Between both firewalls
#         Service : VPN key exchange
# Description : Permit session key exchanges for IBM tunnels
permit FW1 NM FW2 NM udp eq 4001 eq 4001 non-secure local both l=y f=y (5)
permit FW2 NM FW1 NM udp eq 4001 eq 4001 non-secure local both l=y f=y (6)


#       Between H1 and H2
#         Service : VPN traffic 1/2
# Description : Permit routed traffic on secure interface (non-encrypted)
permit H1 NM H2 NM all any 0 any 0 secure route inbound l=y f=y        (7)
permit H2 NM H1 NM all any 0 any 0 secure route outbound l=y f=y       (8)


#       Between H1 and H2
#         Service : VPN traffic 2/2 (tunnel x)
# Description : Permit routed traffic on non-secure interface (encrypted)
permit H1 NM H2 NM all any 0 any 0 non-secure route outbound l=y f=y t=x (9)
permit H2 NM H1 NM all any 0 any 0 non-secure route inbound l=y f=y t=x (10)
```

Figure 45. Filter Rules for Specific Host-to-Host Traffic

This last example leads us to the next scenario, in which we connect two hosts within the secure networks again, but this time we do not trust the secure networks anymore.

Chapter 6. Business Partner/Supplier Network Scenario

This chapter explores an extension of the branch office scenario, the secure connection between two hosts belonging to untrusted intranets over the public Internet. The focus in this scenario expands from protecting your intranets from outside attacks to protecting single hosts within the intranets also from inside attacks.

Consider a situation where a manufacturing company needs to communicate regularly with its suppliers, for example to facilitate just-in-time delivery of parts, to settle invoices among themselves, or for any number of other reasons. There are two issues to consider:

- Access Control: While it may be a business necessity for supplier A to have access to some of company X's internal resources (such as databases), there will also be valid business reasons to prevent the supplier from having access to all of company X's databases.

- Data Confidentiality: Clearly the data should be hidden from general view while it is in transit over the public Internet. But there may be even more stringent requirements. Company X may consider its own intranet to be trusted, but its suppliers may not. For example, a supplier may want to insure that its sensitive data, while traveling through company X's intranet, is hidden until it reaches its final destination. For example, the supplier may be worried that an unscrupulous eavesdropper inside company X may try to intercept the data and sell it to a competitor. And company X may have the same concerns about its data as it travels though the supplier's intranet. Thus, it will not be unusual for each party to treat the other's intranet as untrusted.

6.1 Design Considerations

This scenario is an extension of the multiple branch office scenario. Here we have multiple supplier intranets that need to access a common corporate network over the Internet. Each supplier is allowed access to only a limited set of destinations within the corporate network. Even though traffic from the different suppliers flows over common data links in both the public Internet and in the destination intranet, the VPN must be constructed to guarantee that no traffic from a given supplier will be visible to any other supplier or to any system other than its intended destination.

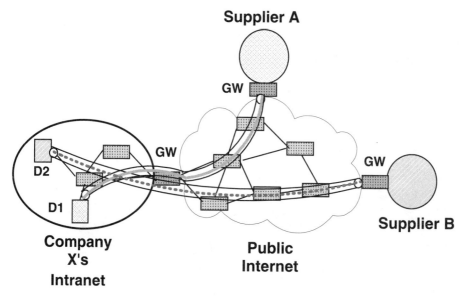

Supplier A

GW

GW

GW

D2

D1

**Company
X's
Intranet**

**Public
Internet**

Supplier B

Figure 46. A Typical Supplier Configuration

Figure 46 illustrates how the two data paths, represented by the dashed and solid lines inside the VPN tunnels, can flow through several common boxes. In this example, supplier A can talk only to destination D1 and supplier B can talk only to destination D2. Traffic from suppliers A and B can be intermixed both within the Internet and within company X's intranet.

IPSec provides a secure solution in this environment, but it will be more complex than for the branch office scenario outlined in Chapter 5, "Branch Office Connection Scenario" on page 89. The extra complexity arises from the following factors:

- There can be multiple suppliers who need to communicate with the manufacturer. Hence, it may be necessary to insure that supplier A can never see any other supplier's data in cleartext form, either in the Internet or in the manufacturer's intranet.

- If the manufacturer and the suppliers, or some subset of them, use private addressing in their respective intranets, then it is possible that *routing collisions* can occur if the same private address has been assigned to multiple hosts. To avoid this possibility, the members of the VPN must either use public IP addresses in their intranets, coordinate the assignment of private IP addresses among the systems participating in the VPN, or adopt some sort of Network Address Translation strategy.

- Because security coverage extends from host-to-host (client-to-server) rather than just from gateway-to-gateway, there will be many more security associations to be negotiated, and many more keys to be securely distributed and refreshed, as compared to the branch office scenario. Hence, the automated secure functions of ISAKMP/Oakley will become even more important.

- Because security coverage extends from host-to-host, IPSec functions will need to be supported in clients, servers, and firewalls.

6.1.1 Authenticating and Encrypting Supplier Traffic

As shown in Figure 47, the VPN gateway that guards the entry to company X's intranet must accept traffic from both supplier A and supplier B. This can be accomplished by using IPSec's AH protocol. There will be one tunnel between the firewall of company X and supplier A and another between the firewall or router of company X and supplier B. The AH protocol will be used in tunnel mode, providing cryptographically strong access control. Therefore systems in supplier intranet A can communicate with destination D1, and systems in supplier intranet B can communicate with destination D2.

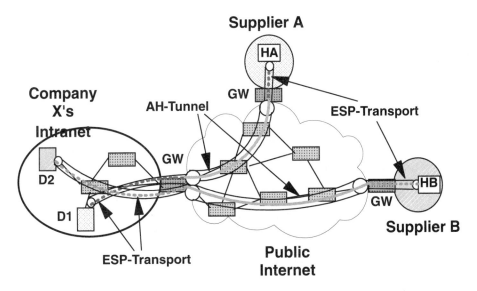

Figure 47. A Typical Supplier Configuration

But as we have noted, there is a need for even finer-grained authentication, namely, each source to its intended destination. For example, in Figure 46 on page 104, we need to assure that destination D1 will accept traffic only from host HA and not from host HB. To achieve data confidentiality, we will use end-to-end encryption between each host and its intended destination server (for example, from host HA to destination D1). IPSec protocols provide the means to accomplish this by using *bundled security associations* (SA bundles), which make use of both tunnel and transport modes of operation simultaneously.

To handle the host-to-host authentication and encryption requirements, we will establish a security association (SA) between each client machine and its server. The protocol will be ESP with authentication, and the type of SA will be transport mode, since this is an end-to-end security association.

Next, we establish a different security association between the gateways that protect company X's intranet and the supplier's intranet. This SA applies over only part of the complete path, so it will use the AH protocol in tunnel mode. Because of tunnel mode, the packet will have the gateway's IP addresses in the "outer" IP header. Therefore also private addresses could be used on the intranets. (See 6.1.2, "Addressing Issues" on page 107 for details.) Between firewalls or routers, ESP security association will be nested inside the AH security association. Figure 48 illustrates the structure of the datagram that flows between firewalls or routers. An inner datagram is nested inside an outer datagram to support two distinct bundled security associations: client-to-server and gateway-to-gateway.

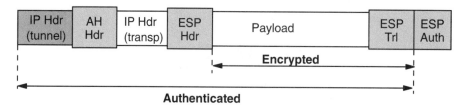

Figure 48. *A Typical Supplier Scenario Datagram*

Note that IPSec protocols enforce two levels of authentication: firewall-to-firewall and client-to-server. The firewall-to-firewall authentication prevents denial-of-service attacks by making sure that only traffic from legitimate suppliers can enter company X's intranet; the host-to-host authentication assures that the destination will accept traffic only from its intended partner machines.

This considerably exacerbates scaling issues. Unlike the branch office case where security associations were established only between VPN firewalls or routers, it is now necessary to establish two additional security associations per client. Each security association will require its own set of cryptographic keys. This scenario illustrates the need for automated ISAKMP-based methods, both for negotiating multiple bundled security associations and for distributing the associated keys.

6.1.2 Addressing Issues

In Figure 47 on page 105 there are tunnels between supplier A and company X, and also between supplier B and company X, but there is no tunnel between supplier A and supplier B. For routing purposes, supplier A and company X will run a mutually acceptable routing protocol over their tunnel, and company X and supplier B will also independently run their own routing protocol. Because each tunnel has its own security association, routing data for supplier A can be kept secret from supplier B, and vice versa. As in the case of the Branch Office Interconnection scenario, each security association will use IPSec's ESP protocol to both encrypt and authenticate the routing updates.

Unlike the Branch Office case, where we could assume that a consistent addressing plan had been applied across all the company's intranets, in this configuration it is very likely that company X and each of its suppliers have administered their own addressing plan independently of one another. For example, it would be possible that supplier A and supplier B both used private (globally ambiguous) IP addresses in their networks, and it would be possible for some or all of their addresses to overlap. In this case, conventional IP routing protocols will not be able to resolve these ambiguities. Hence, we will make the assumption that the IP addresses of all systems, both in the corporate intranet and in the suppliers' intranets, have been assigned so that they are non-overlapping. That is, we will assume that when private IP addresses are used, there will be coordination between the communicating intranets.

Note: As mentioned in 1.3.3.1, "Network Address Translation" on page 15, NAT will not help in this case because it will change IP address information which will cause IPSec authentication to fail. In fact, since we need to build end-to-end IPSec tunnels in this scenario, NAT will prohibit the proper setup of security associations alltogether.

6.1.3 Packet Filtering and Proxies

In this configuration, we have seen that there is a requirement for end-to-end encryption. This can cause problems for conventional packet filtering techniques, since the TCP header is part of the encrypted payload field and is no longer visible to the VPN firewalls or routers. Another area that needs to be addressed is the nesting of IPSec protocols. This means that the VPN firewall or router must be able to handle IP packets where the Next protocol field might indicate AH or ESP. It may also mean that packet filters will need to operate on both "inner" and "outer" IP address information, in cases where tunnel mode is used.

This area needs more study. The effectiveness of packet filtering will be significantly reduced, since unencrypted upper layer data is no longer available for examination by the VPN firewall or router. As the cryptographic techniques become used more widely for end-to-end protection, more and more access control decisions in a firewall will be handled via the AH protocol, and conventional packet filtering will become less and less useful. However, for traditional non-VPN traffic such as everyday World Wide Web access or news, packet filtering will still play its usual role. At the final destination host, where cleartext data is once again available, packet filtering will also continue to play a useful role for providing finer-grained level of access control within the destination host itself.

6.1.4 Summary: Inter-Company Interconnection

This application of IPSec uses the public Internet to connect a company and its suppliers. It requires upgrades to existing client and server machines, since they must now support the IPSec protocol suite. It requires enhancements to conventional packet filtering techniques, because some headers from upper layer protocols may no longer be decryptable at the VPN firewall or router. And finally, it makes use of IPSec's nesting capabilities. The major elements of complexity, compared to the branch office case, are summarized below:

- Client machines (hosts and servers) must support IPSec's ESP protocol, both for encryption and for authentication.

- The number of machines that need to participate in the IPSec protocols has increased significantly. Security associations will need to be set up both end-to-end and gateway-to-gateway.

- For very small configurations, manual key distribution and manual configuration of security associations may be possible, but for any medium to large-sized configuration, support for ISAKMP/Oakley in clients, servers, and VPN-firewalls will rapidly become a necessity.

- New packet filtering rules will need to be developed to accommodate: a) encrypted upper layer payloads, and b) pairs of inner and outer cleartext headers that arise when IPSec protocols are nested within one another. It remains to be seen if firewall or router filtering rules in the presence of end-to-end encryption will continue to serve a useful purpose. In the long term, filtering's importance will probably diminish as cryptography-based access control techniques become more widely used.

6.2 Manual Key Distribution

As we mentioned in Appendix A, "IBM eNetwork VPN Solutions" on page 119 the current IPSec RFCs provide no key management functionality. Therefore, unfortunately, the only short term solution for manual tunnels is manual key distribution. In our opinion this currently limits manual tunnels to small scale implementations. This will change later this year with the introduction of Internet Key Exchange (IKE) (see Chapter 4, "The Internet Key Exchange (IKE) Protocol" on page 71).

6.2.1 Using Mail

Most methods of exchanging keys are non-secure. Cutting and pasting the key into an e-mail message would be the simplest and most efficient manual method of key distribution, but unless the mail is secure itself, it is open to the possibility of being intercepted. Many e-mail packages keep the data in plain text on the host system, or server. This makes the secret key information vulnerable.

Of course sending conventional mail (for instance a diskette containing the keys) is also a valid way but it usually introduces a time problem. Depending on the value for the session key lifetime it could well be that the keys expire before the diskette arrives at your partner's location. You could send many keys at once and later on tell your partner on the phone to change to the second, third or whatever key.

6.2.2 Using Secure Socket Layer (SSL)

A possible means of exchanging keys in a secure manner is the use of a separate encrypted communications channel. An example of an encrypted communications channel is Secure Sockets Layer (SSL). SSL is a client/server based method of secure communication. SSL was developed by Netscape Communications Corporation as an open, non-proprietary protocol.

The SSL client could be for instance Netscape Navigator. For the server, IBM offers the Internet Connection Secure Server (ICSS). ICSS is available under a separate license agreement. For more information on SSL, refer to the following URL: `http://home.netscape.com/assist/security/ssl/index.html`.

6.2.3 Using Pretty Good Privacy (PGP)

Another way to send keys to your partner is by employing *Pretty Good Privacy (PGP)*. PGP is a freely available program that uses public-key cryptography to create encrypted and authenticated messages.

You can download the international version of PGP from `http://www.pgpi.com`. If you are based in the U.S., you should use `http://www.pgp.com`.

For a detailed description on how to use PGP on an RS/6000 see section 7.6 of the IBM redbook *Protect and Survive Using IBM Firewall 3.1 for AIX*, SG24-2577.

6.3 Variations of the Business Partner/Supplier Network Scenario

There are two variations to the business partner/supplier scenario that we could think of but did not elaborate on:

1. The first one is actually the "normal" solution: use of an ESP new header format protocol, which allows authentication within the ESP protocol.

2. The second variation: if both sides use official Internet addresses and do not need to hide their intranet structure, there is no need for a FW-to-FW tunnel. (One would just need the proper filter rules on the firewall.)

Chapter 7. Remote Access Scenario

With the advent of tele-working, remote access to corporate networks is increasingly important these days. The traditional way of deploying modem pools and remote access servers is expensive because of the dedicated equipment needed and especially because of the long-distance telephone costs involved. As the Internet has become virtually omnipresent, just a local phone call away, the remote access costs can be greatly reduced by using the Internet as the access infrastructure to the corporate network.

In this chapter we examine how remote users can exploit IPSec features to establish secured connections to their corporate intranets over the Internet.

For this scenario, let's assume that company A has procured Internet access from an ISP and wants to enable its mobile work force to access the resources located in the corporate network over the Internet. For simplicity we do not consider other possible connections, such as Internet access or other VPN scenarios. These issues can be dealt with separately. The techniques described here can also be applied to secure traditional dial-in connections.

7.1 Design Considerations

The major issue to be addressed is the inherently dynamic nature of this scenario. Typically SAs cannot be pre-configured because the clients' addresses cannot be predicted. ISPs assign addresses dynamically. At some ISPs it is possible to request fixed addresses for dial-in connections, but only at an extra charge.

We need to be able to identify the remote client by its name rather than by its IP address. ISAKMP/Oakley has this ability, but it is not yet implemented in every vendor's products.

To facilitate effective tunnel management, with dynamic tunnels most of the tunnel parameters are auto-generated, much like in the case of IBM tunnels (see A.1.2, "Tunnel Types" on page 121). The filter rules associated with a dynamic tunnel are automatically effective at client connection time and cease operation when the client closes the tunnel. These dynamic filter rules are always checked *before* the static filter rules and cannot be modified. Advantages of this mode of operation are the ease of use and the guaranteed functionality. However, the dynamic filter rules permit all traffic from the client to the whole intranet including the firewall itself and there is no way to change that. The reason behind this is that a remote client normally needs the same access to the resources as if it were actually in the intranet. The security policy for the secure network, not the firewall, is what determines the access for the remote client once connected and authenticated.

If the clients' addresses are known (preassigned by the ISP), then we are not limited to dynamic tunnels and the clients mentioned.

Another important design point is whether to extend IPSec tunnels to the hosts in the intranet or not. Most companies trust their intranets; for them there is no reason to do so. This approach has the advantage of a much smaller number of SAs to be managed. Also, the end systems do not need to be modified to support IPSec.

Sometimes very stringent security regulations are in place and the intranet is untrusted. In this case the IPSec tunnels should go directly to the destination host. IPSec should be deployed to those hosts and a large number of SAs should be managed. These factors could have significant cost and system management implications. A setup like this which is also shown in Figure 31 on page 67 cannot (yet) be facilitated using the current IBM IPSec clients.

Extending a tunnel from the client to the server also could make sense in another, very special situation: when the client is a *foreign* one, for example a traveling business partner's notebook that is allowed to connect to a corporate server. This setup resembles to the business partner/supplier scenario, the difference being that all tunnels originate from the client itself.

7.1.1 Data Confidentiality and Authentication

It is obvious that company A wants the dial-in traffic to be encrypted. Authentication is also needed because the corporate firewall must admit only traffic from the remote clients. Thus, either ESP tunnels with authentication option or combined AH-ESP tunnels should be used.

7.1.2 Addressing and Routing Issues

Unlike in the Branch Office connection or business partner/supplier scenarios, here we have one endpoint of the tunnels in the Internet. The clients will have automatically assigned public IP addresses by the ISP at connect time. These are routable everywhere. The router installed by the ISP at company A's site knows how to route to the Internet. Therefore, the only requirement for the internal routers is to have routes that direct Internet traffic to the corporate firewall, which in turn routes to the ISP's router. This should be the case anyway.

The IPSec code at the dial-in clients should be capable of differentiating between the corporate traffic which is to be tunneled and the ordinary Internet traffic that requires no special treatment. If they sent all traffic through the tunnel, then the remote user would loose the ability to access Internet resources while operating that tunnel, because the firewall normally would drop the packets retrieved from a tunnel that have non-secure source and destination addresses.

The addressing scheme of the intranet needs no modification to support dial-in clients. If the intranet uses private addresses, it will still be reachable, because packets with private IP addresses are tunneled and the tunnel endpoints have public addresses. Only the subnets with direct connection to the Internet need to have public addresses. This is no new requirement.

7.1.3 Multiprotocol Support

If protocols other than IP should be supported for the remote clients, then besides IPSec an appropriate tunneling protocol that will carry the non-IP payload must be supported by the firewall and by the ISP's Point of Presence. However, these protocols do not offer robust cryptographic features comparable to IPSec. Therefore the solution is to use IPSec to protect the traffic that flows in the multiprotocol tunnel.

In this case a viable choice is L2TP which is likely to be supported by more and more ISPs. Note that the non-IP protocol must not only be supported at the remote client and at the destination server, but also at the firewall. Otherwise the firewall would have no means to send the decapsulated non-IP payload to its ultimate destination.

With L2TP, the PPP connection that was in place between the remote client and the ISP is now extended to the corporate firewall. This results in the client and the firewall being on the same IP subnet and allows for the firewall to assign the client's address itself.

7.1.4 Summary: Remote Access

This application of VPN technology replaces existing direct dial-in lines to the corporate network and instead uses the Internet as the access infrastructure. Here are the major design considerations:

- The solution does not require changes at the servers in the corporate network unless the dial-in traffic is to be protected against attacks on the intranet as well. However, clients have to support the IPSec protocols.

- Because client addresses are typically dynamic, the IBM Firewall's dynamic tunnel is the adequate tunnel type. This does not allow for tunnels to extend back to the servers in the corporate intranet, but in practice this is not a great disadvantage.

ISAKMP/Oakley will remove this limitation. Manual tunnels are feasible only with fixed remote client IP addresses.

- The dial-in traffic will be encrypted and authenticated. Any traffic that cannot be authenticated will be rejected by the firewall.

- There are no special routing or addressing issues. Existing intranet addresses can be used "as is".

- Existing packet filtering rules, if any, do not interfere with the dynamic filter rules. They can be used without modification.

- Explicit filter rules to protect the corporate intranet against non-VPN traffic are not required because the IPSec authentication will provide this protection.

Note: We would like to remark here that the term *corporate firewall* used in the previous paragraphs could be replaced with the term *router* if such a box offers equivalent functionality, such as dynamic tunnels or ISAKMP/Oakley.

7.2 An Insight View to Dynamic Tunnels

In this section we describe in detail how an IBM dynamic tunnel (see A.1.2, "Tunnel Types" on page 121) works by following the itinerary of an IP packet from the remote client to the destination host in the intranet.

When the remote client user opens a secure session, the GUI starts an SSL control session with the firewall, using TCP on port 4005. The SSL server application on the firewall authenticates the client based on user ID and password, sends the tunnel keys and policy and activates the dynamic tunnel and dynamic filter rules. After that, the SSL control session is terminated. This traffic is allowed by the SSL from the World connection that translates to the following static filter rules:

```
permit 0 0 0 0 tcp      any    0 eq 4005 both both both l=y
permit 0 0 0 0 tcp/ack  eq  4005 any    0 both both both l=y
```

Now the client can start the tunnel and activate its own filter rules that basically steer the corporate traffic into or out of the tunnel.

The dynamic filter rules activated by the SSL server application on the firewall are listed below. For easier reading we use the following notations:

FW: IP address of the firewall (non-secure interface)

CLI: IP address of the remote client

FF: 255.255.255.255

x: tunnel number

z: 4005

```
permit  FW FF CLI FF tcp eq  z any 0 non-secure local outbound l=y f=y t=0  (1)
permit CLI FF  FW FF esp any 0 any 0 non-secure local inbound  l=y f=y t=0  (2)
permit CLI FF  FW FF ah  any 0 any 0 non-secure local inbound  l=y f=y t=0  (3)
permit CLI FF   0  0 all any 0 any 0 non-secure both  inbound  l=y f=y t=x  (4)
permit   0  0 CLI FF all any 0 any 0 non-secure both  outbound l=y f=y t=x  (5)
permit CLI FF   0  0 all any 0 any 0 secure      route outbound l=y f=y t=0  (6)
permit   0  0 CLI FF all any 0 any 0 secure      route inbound  l=y f=y t=0  (7)
```

Notes:

1. Rule (1) permits the SSL server application to initiate a TCP connection to the specific remote client. Observe that the static filter rules do not allow this.

2. Rules (2) and (3) allow inbound IPSec traffic from the client. These are the "green light" for the encapsulated IP packets.

3. Rules (4) and (5) specify that client traffic should go through the tunnel x in both directions. Rule (4) is applied after the inbound IPSec packet was decapsulated. Rule (5) is applied before the outbound packet is encapsulated and actually instructs the firewall to do this encapsulation.

4. Rules (6) and (7) permit unrestricted bidirectional access to the secure network.

5. On outbound processing the filters are not checked after the IPSec encapsulation, that's why there is no need for a permit rule that allows outbound IPSec packets. Rule (5) is sufficient.

Now let's take a look on the process flow inside the firewall (see Figure 49 on page 116).

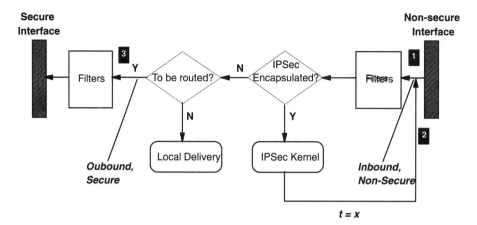

Figure 49. *Inbound Packet Processing by the Firewall*

Suppose that an IPSec packet arrives at the non-secure interface of the firewall, with the destination in the secure network. The tunnel policy is encr/auth, that is, the outer IPSec header is AH. Let's denote dynamic filter rule r by DF(r).

1. The packet attributes are inbound, non-secure. As it is checked against the dynamic filter rules (remember, they are always checked first), a match is found with DF(3), so it passes to the IPSec decapsulation. Using the SPI, the IPSec kernel retrieves the tunnel policy, strips off the IPSec headers, associates the tunnel ID x to the packet and sends it to the filters again.

2. Now DF(4) is matched and the packet proceeds to IP routing check.

3. The packet has to be routed, therefore the filters are checked again, but now the attributes of the packet are outbound, secure. There is a match with DF(6), so the packet is sent to the secure interface, which delivers it to the secure network.

The reverse flow is shown in the figure below.

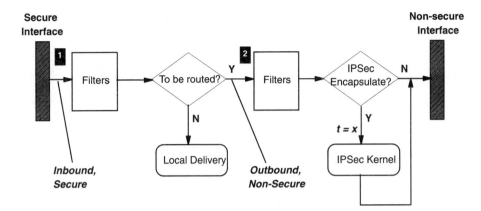

Figure 50. Outbound Packet Processing by the Firewall

A plain IP packet destined to the remote client arrives at the secure interface. Here is what happens:

1. The packet attributes are inbound, secure. At the first rules check DF(7) matches and the packet is accepted.

2. Since this packet has to be routed, the filters are checked again, but now the packet attributes are outbound, non-secure. Now DF(5) matches, and because it indicates a nonzero tunnel ID, the packet is sent to IPSec encapsulation. The IPSec kernel processes the packet based on the tunnel policy that it retrieved using the tunnel ID. The encapsulated packet is not sent to the filters again, it goes directly to the non-secure interface and travels to the client.

When the remote client closes the secure session, the GUI starts another SSL control session with the firewall. The same authentication takes place as in the case of session opening. Then the firewall deactivates the dynamic tunnel and removes the dynamic filter rules for the remote user. The client is notified and the SSL control session is terminated.

Appendix A. IBM eNetwork VPN Solutions

The description of the IBM eNetwork VPN solutions in the following sections lists the implementation of VPN features on the various IBM platforms and positions the different products. Towards the end of the chapter there are two tables. One covers the interoperability between IBM products, the other shows how IBM solutions interoperate with other vendors' VPN products.

A.1 Key Terms and Features

As discussed in Chapter 1, "Virtual Private Networks (VPN) Overview" on page 1 all IBM eNetwork VPN solutions are based on IPSec, because it is the only available framework addressing most of the aforementioned security exposures. Before describing the functions available on the different IBM platforms we need to discuss features and terms commonly used on all platforms.

Note: The IBM Nways router platforms (2210 and 2216) offer layer 2 tunneling functionality (L2TP) and multiprotocol support in addition to IPSec. All those features are described in a separate IBM redbook, *A Comprehensive Guide to Virtual Private Networks, Volume II: IBM Nways Router Solutions*, SG24-5234, to be published later this year.

A.1.1 IPSec Functionality

In this section we discuss all variations found in the IBM eNetwork VPN solutions. However, some products may not offer all options listed. Please refer to Table 1 on page 126 and Table 2 on page 134 for details.

A.1.1.1 IPSec Protocols

The valid security protocols are ESP (RFCs 1827 and 1829) and AH (RFC 1826). Authentication and encryption can be used independently. There are implementations (such as AIX V4.3 and the 2210/2216 Router) that also use headers defined by newer Internet Drafts. (See Chapter 3, "Description of IPSec" on page 47 for an explanation of the differences between the original and the new IPSec headers.)

A.1.1.2 Policies

Your tunnel defined policy specifies that the data (original IP packets) be either:

- Encrypted (encr only)
- Authenticated (auth only)
- Encrypted and then authenticated (encr/auth)

- Authenticated and then encrypted (auth/encr)
- Neither encrypted nor authenticated (none)

The tunnel policy or level of protection depends on your security requirements. A typical scenario may have multiple secure networks (for example, branches of a company that are in different cities) with tunnels between them in order to protect the information. There may be more than one tunnel between a single pair of nodes, which might be useful for different encryption and authentication choices. An example of such a requirement for multiple SAs between nodes is described in Chapter 6, "Business Partner/Supplier Network Scenario" on page 103.

If you use both authentication and encryption we recommend that you use the option encrypted and then authenticated. It will authenticate the full IP datagram, including the encapsulated IP header. The RFCs determine this option as mandatory whereas they do not specify authenticated and then encrypted as a required option. That makes sense because this option would not authenticate the encapsulated IP header.

For more details see Chapter 3, "Description of IPSec" on page 47, and especially 3.4, "Combining IPSec Protocols" on page 62 which outlines common scenarios.

A.1.1.3 Cryptographic Algorithms (Transforms)

Currently the following transforms are used for authentication within the IBM eNetwork VPN solutions:

- KEYED MD5
- HMAC MD5 (with optional replay protection)
- HMAC SHA (with optional replay protection)

The following algorithms are used for encryption/decryption:

- DES CBC 4 (with a 32-bit initialization vector)
- DES CBC 8 (with a 64-bit initialization vector)
- 3DES CBC
- CDMF

> **Note:** With the initial RFCs two packet headers were necessary to provide both authentication and encryption. The new header format drafts offer an ESP header that allows an additional authentication algorithm of your choice (as long it is a transform that uses the new header format). Currently this kind of ESP header can be used in the AIX V4.3 implementation.

A.1.2 Tunnel Types

An IPSec tunnel is defined by specifying a pair of security associations (SAs) between two hosts. A security association is uniquely identified by a triple consisting of a security parameter index (SPI), an IP destination address, and a security protocol (AH or ESP) identifier. The security parameter index (SPI) enables the receiving system to select the security association under which a received packet will be processed. Other elements of the security association (SA) such as the cryptographic algorithms to use, keys and lifetime can be specified, or defaults can be used.

There are two SA types: tunnel mode and transport mode. According to the RFCs firewalls have to use tunnel mode if they are acting as gateways; the implementation of transport mode is optional for firewalls. See Chapter 3, "Description of IPSec" on page 47 for details on IPSec protocols and security associations.

Currently there are three kinds of IPSec tunnels that IBM uses for different purposes in its eNetwork VPN products:

A.1.2.1 Manual Tunnel

A manual tunnel implements the IPSec standards and is typically used between an IBM firewall and a non-IBM firewall. In theory you should be able to use it to connect to any product supporting the IPSec standards. In practice it depends mainly on whether you are able to find a combination of tunnel characteristics (such as transforms, policy and header format) supported by both products. Many vendors offer the transforms keyed MD5 with DES or HMAC MD5 with DES. This is a base subset that works with most implementations of the IPSec RFCs. In our tests we used manual tunnels for instance between an AIX V4.3 server and a Windows 95 system running the eNetwork Communications Suite. (See Chapter 6, "Business Partner/Supplier Network Scenario" on page 103 for the configuration details.)

This tunnel type usually requires all fields to be filled in manually. (Although some products, such as the eNetwork Firewall for AIX, will assign an autogenerated value to some fields; for details see the corresponding product section later in this chapter.)

- Source and destination IP address of the tunnel.

- SA Type: Tunnel or transport mode. If your system acts as a gateway, it has to use tunnel mode. If acting as a host, we recommend that you choose transport mode. It involves less overhead than tunnel mode.

  Note: If you have no such field on a firewall acting as a security gateway, according to the RFCs it has to use tunnel mode. On a client if there is no choice, you may assume that it probably uses transport mode.

- IPSec protocol, policy and authentication/encryption transform: See A.1.1, "IPSec Functionality" on page 119.

- Source and destination key: The keys have to match on both tunnel sides. The value your partner has chosen for the source key is your destination key and vice versa.

- Source and destination SPI: There is one SPI pair for AH and another one for ESP (if you use both protocols). The above rule for the keys goes also for the SPIs; the value your partner specified as source SPI is your destination SPI and vice versa. SPI value 0 is reserved to indicate that no security association exists. The set of SPI values in the range of 1 through 255 are reserved by the Internet Assigned Numbers Authority (IANA) for future use.

- Session key lifetime: Specifies the time in minutes that a manual tunnel will be operational. When the tunnel life time is reached, the tunnel will cease operation until you start it again. Note that after only starting the tunnel again the keys remain the same; for security reasons you should establish new keys. Otherwise the chance for a hacker to crack the key gets bigger as he or she has more time to mount new attacks. The value specified will also affect performance (smaller value, bigger performance hit). Generally, values used for CDMF will be smaller than those used for DES due to the strength of the encryption algorithms.

- Tunnel ID: This value has to uniquely identify the tunnel within the tunnel definitions on your system and must match the ID used in the corresponding tunnel definition of your partner. It is actually not required for the security association but for the packet filter rules. If the tunnel ID does not equal zero, the data packet is sent to the IPSec kernel. This field is not required by the RFCs, but used within all IBM server/gateway products described in this book.

- Replay Prevention: This feature is only available with the new draft header format used for instance by HMAC MD5 and HMAC SHA. Some newer implementations already support replay prevention. For instance, in the AIX V4.3 manual tunnel definition you will find the option of whether you want to use replay prevention or not. If this field exists, make sure that you match your partners definitions or capabilities. If you use keyed MD5, replay prevention is not a valid option.

For manual tunnels the RFCs recommend not to use replay prevention. The reason is that the RFCs do not allow a wrap arround of the counter that is used for replay prevention. Therefore, if the counter reaches its maximum value the tunnel has to cease and must be started again. With a long session key lifetime this situation is likely. (Please see Chapter 3, "Description of IPSec" on page 47 for details.)

The name manual tunnel already implies that there is no automatic key management. As currently there is no key management protocol specified in the IPSec RFCs IBM will include the ISAKMP/Oakley key management protocol later this year when the corresponding RFCs are in place. Until then as long as you use manual tunnels you have to either refresh the keys manually or inhibit key refreshes at all. (Please see 6.2, "Manual Key Distribution" on page 108 for considerations on this topic.) Sometimes this manual key distribution is also referred to as *preshared keys*. Because of the administration overhead currently involved with manual tunnels for the short term we recommend you use IBM tunnels whenever possible. They offer a solution to the key refresh issue.

A.1.2.2 IBM Tunnel

This kind of tunnel uses IP Security Protocol (IPSP) which is an IBM unique protocol. It features an automatic key update mechanism, using UDP port 4001. Under this scheme, a new encryption key is generated at regular intervals and communicated through the tunnel encrypted under the current key. With IBM tunnels there is no need (and in fact also no option) to specify the SPIs and the keys; they are automatically determined by the software. There is also no choice for the authentication algorithm; IBM tunnels always use keyed MD5. On the other hand you have to specify options not found in a manual tunnel definition.

Besides some of the fields discussed in the manual tunnel section above (tunnel ID, source and destination IP address, policy and ESP transform), you will find the following additional fields when defining an IBM tunnel:

- Initiator: Determines who starts the session negotiation. If you are not sure what your partner has specified, set it to yes. If both partners specify yes, the tunnel logic will resolve the deadlock. If no partner sets it to yes, the tunnel will not operate at all.

- Session Key Lifetime: This field is very similar to the one described in the section on manual tunnels. It specifies the time in minutes where the current session key may be used. The big difference is, however, that a new key will be automatically created before the old key expires. Therefore, the IBM tunnel does not cease operation after the key lifetime has elapsed.

- Session Key Refresh Time: Specifies the time in minutes between a new key start and an old key expiration. If for instance the refresh time is 10 minutes, then the old and the new key are both valid during the last 10 minutes of the session key lifetime. Therefore the value must be equal or less than the session key lifetime. The key refresh time should be half of the session key lifetime.

As the name implies already this tunnel type was developed for use with IBM products. Currently it allows, for instance, to establish a connection between two AIX systems (could be AIX firewalls and/or AIX V4.3 systems).

We used the IBM tunnel extensively between AIX firewalls. It is convenient for administrators because they don't need to worry about the key refresh.

A.1.2.3 Dynamic Tunnel

A dynamic tunnel is a special variation of a manual tunnel and is an implementation only found on the IBM firewall. It also uses the IPSec standards, but there are only two IBM clients it is used with:

- Windows 95 IPSec Client (supplied with the eNetwork Firewall for AIX)

- OS/2 TCP/IP V4.1 IPSec Client (part of the OS/2 TCP/IP V4.1 stack)

The reason for calling the tunnel dynamic is that the tunnel definition is not based on the client's IP address but on a client target user. Therefore the client's IP address does not have to be known. This is important because a remote client usually uses a dynamic IP address supplied by the provider when connecting through the Internet to the firewall.

The connection is established by using the Secure Sockets Layer (SSL) protocol. The firewall destination port is 4005. The dynamic tunnel on the firewall is not activated until the client starts the tunnel. When the user selects **Connect tunnel**, the client starts an SSL control session with the firewall. The SSL server application authenticates the remote client based on the (already encrypted) user ID and password and sends the tunnel policy to the client. Because the client IP address is not known by the time of the tunnel definition the necessary firewall filter rules to connect to the secure network are also generated dynamically by the firewall when the tunnel is started by the client.

Note: The dynamic filter rules are put at the top of all filter rules and hence are evaluated first. This also means that on the firewall you have no possibility (as you have with the other tunnel types) to further restrict the traffic between the client and the secure network.

After the tunnel startup the SSL control session is terminated and the user is now able to work with systems on the secure network. The dynamic filters remain active until the user at the client disconnects the tunnel or the tunnel times out.

When the user selects **Disconnect tunnel**, the client starts a new SSL control session with the firewall. The SSL server application authenticates the client again based on user ID and password and deactivates the dynamic tunnel, dynamic filters, and dynamic policy for the remote user. Then the SSL control session is terminated.

The only special field in the definition of a dynamic tunnel is the Target User field. As discussed above it replaces the destination IP address found in the manual tunnel. All other fields were already described in A.1.2.1, "Manual Tunnel" on page 121.

Now that you know what tunnel types IBM uses in its products we have a look at some other functions related to VPNs.

Notes:

1. Keep in mind that IBM's manual tunnel is the one that corresponds to the RFCs. Therefore this is the tunnel type to use if your partner uses a vendor product. The other two tunnel types are solely for use with IBM products.

2. IBM has announced that it will offer standard-compliant automatic key exchange and refresh capabilities for its eNetwork VPN solutions later this year.

A.1.3 Other Important Features

In order to build your VPN solution some other features may be required or helpful:

Packet Filtering
> Packet filtering will help you to restrict VPN traffic to certain systems in your own or your suppliers/business partners network. It is helpful if packet filters are used together with logging.

Logging
> Logging allows you to learn more about what happened to the data packets and about the current VPN status.

IPv6 Support
> For the future it will also be important to know whether a product supports IPv6.

Modular Support for New Cryptographic Transforms
> As the cryptographic algorithms are under continuous improvement it is desirable that the design of the VPN products allows plug-in and replaceable kernel modules for encryption and authentication.

We have included the above features in our evaluations. You will find the results in the specific product sections.

A.2 Server/Gateway Platforms

Based on typical usage we decided to put the following products in this category:

- eNetwork Firewall for AIX V3
- AIX V4.3
- 2210 Nways Multiprotocol Router and 2216 Nways Multiaccess Connector
- OS/390 Server
- 3746 Multiaccess Enclosure

Note: On the Windows NT and AS/400 platforms the IBM firewall products do not yet implement VPN/IPSec functionality but will do so later this year.

The following table reflects the features discussed at the beginning of this chapter. In addition we included other general VPN related product information in the product sections. The interoperability test section later in this chapter lists configuration options we recommend in order to set up a connection between two products.

Table 1 (Page 1 of 2). *IBM Server Platforms - Supported VPN Features (as of June, 1998)*

Feature		eNetwork Firewall for AIX	AIX V4.3	2210 / 2216 / 3746	OS/390 Server
Tunnel Type	IBM	√	√		
	Manual	√	√	√	√
	Dynamic	√			
IPSec Protocol	AH	√	√	√	√
	ESP	√	√	√	√
Header Format	RFCs 18xx	√	√		√
	New Draft Headers		√	√	
SA Type	Transport Mode		√	√	
	Tunnel Mode	√	√	√	√
AH Transform	Keyed MD5	√	√		√
	HMAC MD5		√	√	
	HMAC SHA		√	√	

Table 1 (Page 2 of 2). IBM Server Platforms - Supported VPN Features (as of June, 1998)					
Feature		**eNetwork Firewall for AIX**	**AIX V4.3**	**2210 / 2216 / 3746**	**OS/390 Server**
ESP Transform	DES CBC 4	√	√		√
	DES CBC 8	√	√	√	√
	CDMF	√	√	√	√
	3DES CBC		√ (V4.3.1)	√	
	Authentication		√	√ (optional)	
Other	Packet Filters	√	√	√	√
	Logging	√	√	√ (remote)	√
	Plug-ins		√		
	IP Version 6		√		

> **Important!**
>
> The IBM eNetwork Firewall for AIX and for Windows NT will provide VPN support according to the latest standards and will also include IKE in 1999. Those releases are, at the time of writing, scheduled for release in 1999.
>
> IKE will also become available in 1999 for the AIX, OS/390 and OS/400 servers and for the IBM 2210 and 2216 router platforms.

A.2.1 IBM eNetwork Firewall for AIX

To the best of our knowledge the eNetwork Firewall for AIX was the first IBM product to offer an IPSec implementation (in SNG V.2.1, which was available in October 1995).

We have used the eNetwork Firewall for AIX in several scenarios. See Chapter 5, "Branch Office Connection Scenario" on page 89 for details on how to configure an IBM tunnel between two AIX firewalls. For information on how to set up the eNetwork Firewall for AIX in general we recommend the IBM redbook *Protect and Survive Using IBM Firewall 3.1 for AIX*, SG24-2577.

Currently the AIX V4.3 operating system offers richer VPN functionality than the eNetwork Firewall for AIX. Therefore the IPSec functionality of AIX V4.3.1 will be included in the eNetwork Firewall for AIX later this year.

A.2.1.1 Product Versions

Since the last program services for the Secured Network Gateway (SNG) V2.2 will end on June 24, 1998, we did not include this version in our tests. Concerning VPN features (such as protocols, transforms and policies) SNG V2.2 is identical to the functionality found in AIX firewall V3.1. If you still use SNG V2.2, please make sure that you have applied the latest available service level.

From a functional VPN point of view the eNetwork Firewall for AIX V.3.2 is almost identical to V.3.1. The Win95 IPSec client has changed as discussed in A.3.2.3, "eNetwork Firewall for AIX V3.2" on page 137, reflecting enhancements to the remote user authentication methods.

In eNetwork Firewall for AIX V3.1 some VPN-related defects have been discovered. At the time of writing this redbook all known VPN defects have been fixed in V3.1.1.5 (which was the current code level at that time) and we had no problems after we upgraded our machines to this level of code. Therefore we strongly recommend you upgrade your firewall to the latest available level if you plan to use VPN features. We also used eNetwork Firewall for AIX V.3.2.1 in some scenarios.

A.2.1.2 VPN Features

The eNetwork Firewall for AIX currently offers:

- Tunnel types: All (IBM, manual and dynamic)

- SA Type: Tunnel Mode

  There is no option to choose between tunnel or transport mode; the firewall will always automatically use tunnel mode.

- IPSec protocols: All (AH and ESP)

- Header Formats: RFCs 18xx

- Policies: All (auth, encr, encr/auth, auth/encr)

- AH transform: Keyed MD5

- ESP transforms: DES CBC 4, DES CBC 8 and CDMF

- Other VPN-related features: Packet filtering and logging

A.2.1.3 Hints on Options and Manual Tunnels

The eNetwork Firewall for AIX currently does not support the following options:

- Replay prevention
- Tunnel life time of 0 (unlimited)

This is important to know if your tunnel partner offers this options, such as an AIX V4.3 system which offers both options.

The eNetwork Firewall for AIX creates the values for the SPIs and the keys automatically and puts them in the export files of the tunnel definition. If your partner product has no option for importing a tunnel definition from the firewall, you still need to export the tunnel definitions and have a look at the key and SPI values of the corresponding export files. This will enable you to match them in your partner product's tunnel definition.

A.2.2 AIX V4.3

Starting with AIX V4.3 the operating system offers a rich set of VPN features. With its included packet filtering and logging functionality it could even be used as an entry firewall.

If you are on an AIX V4.3.0 system we recommend you upgrade to AIX V4.3.1. It offers additional VPN functions. See A.2.2.6, "AIX V4.3.1 - New Functions" on page 132 for details on what exactly has changed.

For details on what has changed between AIX V4.2 and AIX V4.3 we recommend the IBM redbook *AIX Version 4.3 Differences Guide*, SG24-2014.

A.2.2.1 VPN Features

AIX V4.3.1 offers:

- Tunnel types: IBM and manual

- SA Types: All (tunnel and transport mode)

- IPSec protocols: All (AH and ESP)

- Header Formats: All (RFCs 18xx and new draft headers)

- Policies: All (auth, encr, encr/auth, auth/encr)

- AH transforms: All (Keyed MD5, HMAC MD5 and HMAC SHA)

- ESP transforms: All (DES CBC 4, DES CBC 8, CDMF, 3DES CBC and the new ESP authentication)

With the initial RFCs two packet headers were necessary to provide both authentication and encryption. The new ESP header format drafts offer an ESP header that allows an additional authentication algorithm of your choice (as long as it is a transform that uses the new header format).

- Other VPN-related features: All (packet filtering, logging, plug-ins and IPv6)

A.2.2.2 Running the Firewall Software on AIX V4.3

AIX V4.3 IPSec interoperates with the eNetwork Firewall for AIX. Although both the firewall and AIX V4.3 support IPv4, firewall code supersedes the AIX IPSec code in providing IPv4 secure tunnel support. This means that if a firewall is configured on a V4.3 system, IPv4 will use the firewall IPSec code. Note that files belonging to the AIX IPSec fileset are unique, so both products can be installed without overwriting each other's files. If AIX IPv4 detects that firewall code is installed, it does not load its own IPSec Version 4 code.

eNetwork Firewall for AIX V3.2 is the first release officially supported on AIX V4.3. Firewall V3.1 does not work on AIX V4.3 and is therefore not supported.

A.2.2.3 Hints on Policies

The SMIT IPSec panels presented in AIX V4.3.0 do not offer the full functionality found on the command line. The following configurations are valid and worked in our manual tunnel tests, but can only be configured by using the command line (or by changing a tunnel that was created via SMIT, using the chtun command):

- Policy encr/auth (also called ea)
- Policy encr only (also called e) with the old RFC headers

In AIX V4.3.1 the SMIT panels for tunnel creation show the same behavior, but the full functionality is now also offered in the SMIT panels for changing tunnel definitions. Before AIX V4.3.1 you needed to use the command line to achieve this. The reason for this somewhat complicated kind of implementation lies in the rich functionality of AIX V4.3 IP Security, which makes it difficult to have a simple SMIT panel structure without loosing some valid combinations.

A.2.2.4 Host-Firewall-Host Tunnel Option

This is a special option we only found on the AIX V4.3 platform. It allows you to establish a tunnel between your AIX V4.3 local host (H1) and a remote firewall (G2) and automatically creates the filter rules needed on your AIX 4.3 system to connect to your real destination host (H2) or network behind the remote firewall. Figure 51 on page 131 illustrates the above scenario.

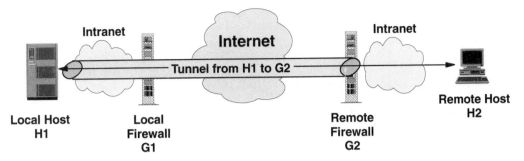

Figure 51. Host-Firewall-Host Tunnel

In our opinion you will rarely need to use this option. It means that you don't trust your own secure network (therefore establishing one tunnel endpoint on your local host), but you trust your partner's secure network (therefore making the remote firewall the other endpoint of the tunnel). The traffic within your partners secure network would then be in cleartext. Given the above case you would then probably also trust your own secure network. Therefore the tunnel endpoints would be the firewalls on both sides and not the endpoints of the real traffic. This setup coincides with our branch office scenario described in Chapter 5, "Branch Office Connection Scenario" on page 89.

The host-firewall-host option makes sense if your tunnel partner has an AIX 4.3 server and you do not trust his or her secure network. In this case your tunnel would have your firewall and the remote AIX server as end points. Your partner would then need to use this option for his or her configuration (if he or she trusts your secure network, that is). If you do not trust the secure networks at all, the business partner/supplier scenario described in Chapter 6, "Business Partner/Supplier Network Scenario" on page 103 is the one you will probably use.

From a technical point of view the host-firewall-host option is actually not about the tunnel definition but the filter definitions. For achieving the same functionality as with the host-firewall-host option you could as well use the host-host option and specify the needed filter rules on the advanced SMIT IPSec panels. Therefore it is just an additional option for your convenience; don't get confused by it.

A.2.2.5 Hints on Manual and IBM Tunnels

AIX V4.3 does not offer a field to enter a tunnel ID. The tunnels are automatically numbered (starting by 1). If your partner uses the tunnel ID field, you have to take care that the auto-generated IDs are not already in use on his or her system.

When entering the keys for manual tunnels, don't forget to put 0x in front of the key. SMIT expects to get a hexadecimal value.

Session key refresh is not supported for IPv6 tunnels.

A.2.2.6 AIX V4.3.1 - New Functions

The new AIX version offers enhanced VPN functionality:

- New transform: Triple DES encapsulation (included in AIX Version 4.3 Bonus Pack for the U.S.).

- Increased options in pairing of authentication and encapsulation algorithms.

  Note: When using the combined ESP header, AIX V4.3.1 allows any AH/ESP combination as long as it uses the new header format. Only keyed MD5 and DES CBC 4 are not able to use the new header format.

- Performance improvements in both HMAC-SHA and DES for PowerPC-based platforms.

- Crypto extensions can be dynamically loaded and unloaded.

- Improved logging: For instance, authentication violations are logged now.

A.2.3 IBM Nways Routers

The current common code base for the IPSec functionality is:

- 2210 Router: Multiprotocol Routing Services (MRS) V3.1

- 2216 Router: Nways Multiprotocol Access Services (MAS) V3.1

A.2.3.1 VPN Features

The two router families offer:

- Tunnel type: Manual

- SA Types: All (tunnel and transport mode)

- IPSec protocols: All (AH and ESP)

- Header Formats: New draft headers

- Policies: All (auth, encr, encr/auth, auth/encr)

- AH transforms: HMAC MD5 and HMAC SHA

- ESP transforms: DES CBC 8, CDMF, 3DES, and the new ESP authentication

- Other VPN-related features: Packet filtering and remote logging

Volume II of the IBM VPN redbooks deals with the VPN implementation in IBMs router products. Please see *A Comprehensive Guide to Virtual Private Networks, Volume II: IBM Nways Router Solutions*, SG24-5234, to be published later this year.

A.2.4 IBM 3746 Multiaccess Enclosure

As the 3746 MAE is also common code based, it supports the same IPSec features that the 2210 and 2216 Nways routers support. These functions were announced May 5, 1998 with a planned general availability of October 30, 1998.

A.2.5 OS/390 Server

The IPSec functionality on an OS/390 Server is based on the eNetwork Communications Server for OS/390, V2R5.

A.2.5.1 VPN Features

Currently an OS/390 Server offers:

- Tunnel types: Manual
- SA Types: Tunnel Mode
- IPSec protocols: All (AH and ESP)
- Header Formats: RFCs 18xx
- Policies: All (auth, encr, encr/auth, auth/encr)
- AH transforms: Keyed MD5
- ESP transforms: DES CBC 4, DES CBC 8 and CDMF
- Other VPN-related features: Packet filtering and logging.

Support for transport mode tunnels will be added in the next release of eNetwork Communications Server for OS/390. For further information on OS/390 Server please see the IBM redbook *Stay Cool on OS/390: Installing Firewall Technology*, SG24-2046.

A.3 Client Platforms

This section covers the IBM VPN client products. Of course systems described in the server section can also be used as VPN clients. Actually from the VPN point of view there is no server and client, but a tunnel owner and partner. If you compare the following feature table to the server table, you will realize additional check boxes to indicate whether the product has dial-up capabilities and/or LAN connectivity. We named the corresponding rows LAN and Dial-up.

None of the clients in the table below supports the IBM tunnel (as it was developed for firewall-to-firewall VPNs) or the more advanced algorithms (HMAC SHA, DES CBC MD5 and 3DES); therefore we removed those features from the client table.

Note: IBM has plans to provide advanced algorithms and new header formats, along with support for automatic key exchange and refresh, also on client platforms later this year.

The following products are covered by the table below:

- AIX IPSec Client (supplied with the eNetwork Firewall for AIX)
- Windows 95 IPSec Client (supplied with the eNetwork Firewall for AIX)
- OS/2 TCP/IP V4.1 IPSec Client (part of the OS/2 TCP/IP V4.1 stack)
- Windows 95 eNetwork Communications Suite V1.1

Table 2 (Page 1 of 2). IBM/OEM Client Platforms - Supported VPN Features (as of June 1998)

Feature		AIX IPSec Client	Windows 95 IPSec Client	OS/2 TCP/IP V4.1	Windows 95 Comms Suite
Tunnel Type	Manual	√		√	√
	Dynamic		√	√	
IPSec Protocol	AH	√	√	√	√
	ESP	√	√	√	√
Header Format	RFCs 18xx	√	√	√	√
	New Draft Headers				
SA Type	Transport Mode			√	√
	Tunnel Mode	√	√	√	√ (ESP only)
AH Transform	Keyed MD5	√	√	√	√
	HMAC MD5				√
ESP Transform	DES CBC 4	√	√		√
	DES CBC 8	√	√		√
	CDMF	√	√	√	

Table 2 (Page 2 of 2). IBM/OEM Client Platforms - Supported VPN Features (as of June 1998)

Feature		AIX IPSec Client	Windows 95 IPSec Client	OS/2 TCP/IP V4.1	Windows 95 Comms Suite
Connectivity	LAN	√		√	√
	Dial-up		√	√	√
Other	Packet Filters	limited		√	
	Logging			√	
	IP Version 6				√

Important!

The IBM eNetwork Firewall for AIX and for Windows NT will provide VPN clients for Windows NT, Windows 95 and Windows 98, which will support IPSec according to the latest standards, including IKE, in 1999.

IKE will also become available in 1999 for the AIX and OS/2 platforms.

A.3.1 AIX IPSec Client (Supplied with the eNetwork Firewall for AIX)

Because the functionality found on an AIX V4.3 system is much better than the one provided in the AIX IPSec Client we recommend you use AIX V4.3 whenever possible. This means use the AIX IPSec Client only if you have to use an AIX level below V4.3.

A.3.1.1 VPN Features

The AIX IPSec Client offers:

- Tunnel types: Manual

- SA Types: Tunnel

- IPSec protocols: All (AH and ESP)

- Header Formats: RFCs 18xx

- Policies: All (auth, encr, encr/auth, auth/encr)

- AH transforms: Keyed MD5

- ESP transforms: DES CBC 4, DES CBC 8 and CDMF

- Connectivity: LAN

- Other VPN-related features: Limited packet filters

Please refer to section 7.4 of the IBM redbook *Protect and Survive Using IBM Firewall 3.1 for AIX, SG24-2577* for a description of how to install the AIX IPSec Client.

A.3.2 Windows 95 IPSec Client (Supplied with the eNetwork Firewall for AIX)

This client is exclusively used with the eNetwork Firewall for AIX. It has two big advantages:

- No requirement for a static IP address on the client.

- eNetwork Firewall for AIX provides it free of charge.

If the above is not important to you or if you need LAN connectivity, the eNetwork Communications Suite might be a better alternative.

A.3.2.1 VPN Features

The Windows 95 IPSec Client includes the following VPN features:

- Tunnel types: Dynamic

- SA Types: Tunnel

- IPSec protocols: All (AH and ESP)

- Header Formats: RFCs 18xx

- Policies: All (auth, encr, encr/auth, auth/encr)

- AH transforms: Keyed MD5

- ESP transforms: DES CBC 4, DES CBC 8 and CDMF

- Connectivity: Dial-up

- Other VPN-related features: None

A.3.2.2 Remote Dial-Up

The client does not tie you to a specific PPP server. The IP address that is assigned by your ISP is irrelevant. The client can support any dial-up Internet provider that offers support for the Password Authentication Protocol (PAP) or the Microsoft

Challenge Handshake Authentication Protocol (MS-CHAP). CompuServe is not supported by the Windows 95 IPSec client.

You can change PPP server and IP addresses and it does not affect the operation of the Windows 95 IPSec Client. Other vendors are sensitive to the specific TCP/IP address; if you change the address, you must reconfigure your client.

In order to establish a connection you first dial into your Internet Service Provider (ISP). Then you log on to the firewall. An encrypted secure login is provided for the Windows 95 IPSec Client using Secure Sockets Layer (SSL) Version 2 technology.

After the tunnel is established, all IP traffic flows through the tunnel. Once users make a connection, they have full TCP/IP access to whatever servers are behind the firewall and can use, among others, FTP, telnet, HTTP, and mail applications.

When using the Windows 95 IPSec client, set the domain name server entry to the server responsible for the name resolution of the the secure network. Otherwise you cannot resolve host names of that network (unless official IP addresses are used within the secure network).

A.3.2.3 eNetwork Firewall for AIX V3.2
The Windows 95 IPSec client in firewall V3.2 has changed as follows:

1. Strong user authentication is now available (it now supports the same security mechanism as the firewall) using Security Dynamics ACE/SecurID cards and tokens.

2. Redesigned client interface.

3. More status information.

Please refer to section 7.7 of the IBM redbook *Protect and Survive Using IBM Firewall 3.1 for AIX, SG24-2577* for a description of how to install the Windows 95 IPSec Client.

A.3.3 OS/2 TCP/IP V4.1 IPSec Client
The VPN implementation is very similar to the Windows 95 IPSec Client as far as the dynamic tunnel type is concerned. Using this feature, the OS/2 TCP/IP V4.1 IPSec Client acts as a tunnel partners to the eNetwork Firewall for AIX. The client is not provided with the firewall but with the OS/2 TCP/IP V4.1 stack.

There is no interface provided to configure manual tunnels with the OS/2 TCP/IP V4.1 IPSec Client. However, you can manually change the tunnel definition, policy and filter files to facilitate that. In fact, the OS/2 IPSec kernel could then behave like a mini-firewall supporting manual tunnels.

TCP/IP V4.1 for OS/2 is available as an update via Software Choice from the following Web Site:

`http://service.software.ibm.com/asd-bin/doc/index.htm`

Note: TCP/IP V4.1 for OS/2 is supported on OS/2 Warp 4, OS/2 Warp Server and OS/2 Warp Server SMP. It requires the following components to be installed prior to its own installation:

1. OS/2 Feature Installer V1.2.1, or higher
2. Netscape Navigator V2.02e for OS/2, or later
3. Java V1.1.4 for OS/2

All of those components are also available via Software Choice.

A.3.3.1 VPN Features

The OS/2 TCP/IP V4.1 IPSec Client offers:

- Tunnel types: Dynamic, manual

- SA Types: Tunnel, transport

- IPSec protocols: All (AH and ESP)

- Header Formats: RFCs 18xx

- Policies: All (auth, encr, encr/auth, auth/encr)

- AH transforms: Keyed MD5

- ESP transforms: CDMF

    Note: The OS/2 TCP/IP V4.1 IPSec Client has been designed to also support DES CBC 4 and DES CBC 8 transforms, but because TCP/IP V4.1 is available as an update via the World Wide Web for which there is no reliable tracking of the origin of a request, the strong encryption module has been removed to comply with U.S. government export restrictions.

- Connectivity: LAN and Dial-up

- Other VPN-related features: Packet filtering and logging

A.3.3.2 Packet Filters

Packet filtering is required to drive the data through the IPSec device drivers. Full packet filtering is possible but only a subset of this function is exposed by TCP/IP V4.1 via the VPN configuration panels.

A.3.3.3 Domain Name Resolution

The client offers a nice feature to solve the problem of how to resolve names in the remote secure network. There are extra fields on the configuration panel to specify the domain and server name for the remote secure network.

A.3.4 Windows 95 eNetwork Communications Suite V1.1

This client offers an implementation of the manual tunnel type for both a LAN and a dial-up environment. These are also the the two main differentiators to the Windows 95 IPSec Client supplied by the eNetwork Firewall for AIX, which implements the dynamic tunnel in a dial-up environment only.

A.3.4.1 Versions

There are two versions of the product:

1. International export version

2. U.S. export controlled version

Because DES is the only supported ESP transform with this client, there is no encryption in the international export version since DES is generally not allowed outside the U.S. and Canada.

A.3.4.2 VPN Features

The eNetwork Communications Suite offers:

- Tunnel types: Manual

- SA Types: All (tunnel and transport mode)

- IPSec protocols: All (AH and ESP)

- Header Formats: RFCs 18xx

- Policies: All important ones (auth, encr, encr/auth)

- AH transforms: Keyed MD5 and HMAC MD5

- ESP transforms: DES CBC 4 and DES CBC 8

- Connectivity: LAN and Dial-in

- Other VPN related features: IPv6

A.3.4.3 Hints

All values entered on the configuration panel are hexadecimal numbers. This includes SPIs which are for instance decimal on an AIX V4.3 system. Therefore you will have to convert the SPIs to decimal numbers before entering them for instance on the AIX V4.3 system.

You will have to reboot the Windows 95 system whenever a new tunnel is added or an existing tunnel is changed.

A.4 Interoperability between IBM VPN Solutions and Other Vendors

If you talk about VPNs, particularly if your VPN extends to your business partners, you may be confronted with the issue of interoperability: does your VPN equipment work with other vendors' VPN-enabled products? While the IPSec standards go a long way towards fostering interoperability, the fact that two different implementations conform to IPSec doesn't necessarily mean that they will interoperate with one another. No standard ever nails down all the details, and like most standards, IPSec provides for a mix of mandatory and optional features.

The IPSec Bakeoffs provide a means for vendors to informally test their IPSec implementations' interoperability, and to iron out any differences in interpretation of the relevant IPSec standards. The most recent IPSec Bakeoff was held in Binghamton, NY, in October 1998. IBM participated with its eNetwork Firewall, AIX, OS/390 and AS/400 servers, and its 2210/2216 Router products. At the time of writing, interoperability information was not yet available.

At an earlier Bakeoff, held in Cary, NC, in March 1998, where IBM participated with its eNetwork Firewall for AIX, AIX V4.3, OS/390 Server and 2210/2216 Router products, IBM VPN solutions interoperated successfully with implementations from many vendors, such as: Frontier Technologies, Cisco, Ascend, Watchguard, Cylan, NIST, Red Creek, Ashley Laurent, Toshiba, Hewlett-Packard, Radguard, Sun, 3Com, Intel, V-One, SEI, Secure Computing, Internet Devices, and Interlink.

Bakeoffs are informal affairs, and the functions provided for testing may be at any stage of development, from early prototypes, to beta code, to fully released commercial products. Testing is usually done in pairs, and each vendor decides what functions it considers most important to evaluate. The results of the informal Bakeoff testing are then fed back to the IPSec Working Group, which uses that input as the basis for refining and clarifying the IPSec protocol standards.

Appendix B. Troubleshooting Your VPN

This chapter helps you in solving IPSec-related problems. We grouped this chapter in a general hints section that we think is valid for all products and information on the specific products. The more general hints of this chapter have been also partly included in Appendix A, "IBM eNetwork VPN Solutions" on page 119 as long as we thought the information is important enough to justify the duplication.

B.1 General Hints

This section summarizes our general experiences and the lessons we have learned.

B.1.1 Double-Check the Field Entries

The most probable cause of a non-working tunnel are field entries that do not match the values entered on the partner system. Remember that your source addresses, SPIs and keys are reflected in the corresponding destination fields of your partners tunnel definition.

Some products, for instance, require a hexadecimal value for the SPI while others expect to receive a decimal number. In this case you have to manually convert the numbers before comparing it to your partners definition.

Of course both tunnel partners need to use the same protocols, header formats, transforms and policies.

B.1.2 Packet Filters

You have to take care that your VPN services go to the top of the filter file (for instance /etc/security/fwfilters.cfg on a eNetwork Firewall for AIX). Otherwise it might well be that other filter rules are evaluated before the VPN services permit or deny traffic that you intend to send through your tunnel.

You should understand the way of a packet described in 5.2, "How Does It Work?" on page 94; this will help you analyze problems.

B.1.3 Logging

The log files are among the most valuable tools in overcoming IPSec-related problems.

However, a logged packet containing a tunnel ID does not guarantee that the packet has been sent from the firewall to the other tunnel partner. It only tells you that the firewall code has sent the packet to the IPSec kernel. If the tunnel partners do not talk to each other, the IPSec kernel will not send the packet. You are able to see this if you trace the connection. You will see a logged packet in the log file but no corresponding packet in the IP trace.

If you see a log entry for the encrypted or authenticated packet leaving your system (non-secure outbound), then the tunnel packet has really been sent out. Unfortunately, some systems, such as the eNetwork Firewall for AIX, do not log this packet.

B.1.4 Nested Tunnels

If you work with nested tunnels, you should first try to get the tunnel between the firewalls to work. After that give the nested tunnel a try.

B.2 Tracing an IPSec Connection

It is often useful to actually see the packets that make up an IPSec connection. You do not have to have specialized network analyzer hardware to do that. Most TCP/IP implementations have a tracing capability, either in the form of commands, for instance iptrace and ipreport on AIX, or iptrace and ipformat on OS/2, or GUI applications, such as IPTrace from the eNetwork Communications Suite and Windows NT Network Monitor.

Apart from IPTrace of the eNetwork Communications Suite and iptrace on OS/2 TCP/IP V4.1, common IP trace tools do not yet recognize IPSec protocols. However, you can look for the protocol numbers 50 (0x32) for AH and 51 (0x33) for ESP in the IP headers. In the case of nested protocols, you will not be able to easily analyze the encapsulated packet. You can recognize for example ESP encapsulated in AH by identifying protocol number 51 in the outer header and by looking for garbled payload data. The tools mentioned do not give a field-by-field breakdown of the inner headers, but if they are not encrypted, you could do it manually.

A more versatile tool is the Windows NT Network Monitor. It has quite sophisticated analyzer features, not limited to IP. With the version of Network Monitor that comes with Microsoft SMS, you can even capture packets of arbitrary destination and source addresses. However, the current version of Network Monitor does not recognize IPSec protocols either.

Notes:

1. Network Monitor will not work in capture mode unless your network adapter and driver support *promiscuous mode*; that is, it can receive LAN frames for any destination, not just those addressed to itself. For example, the IBM LANStreamer family of adapters can be put in promiscuous mode.

2. Network Monitor actually captures LAN data link frames, not just upper layer packets. The data link headers inserted before the IP packets are also shown.

We have used Network Monitor throughout the following sections for convenience as well as for illustration purposes, even though the NT system itself did not have any IPSec capabilities.

B.2.1 Trace Examples

Below we give one example of plain TCP/IP traffic and three examples of captured IPSec traffic. We used Network Monitor to verify the operation of a firewall-firewall IPSec tunnel in the scenario described in Chapter 5, "Branch Office Connection Scenario" on page 89. Follow the steps below to trace an IPSec connection:

1. Plug in the Network Monitor machine in a subnet that is crossed by the IPSec tunnel to be traced.

2. Define a filter that captures only IP traffic between the tunnel endpoints. See the Network Monitor documentation and help on how to do this.

3. Start the capture.

4. Generate some known traffic that goes through the tunnel; for example, open a telnet session, issue commands that list something, etc.

5. Stop the capture and save it. Then open the saved file for analysis.

B.2.1.1 Example 1: Plain TCP/IP Connection

Figure 52 on page 144 shows the trace of a plain TCP/IP connection between the firewalls systems 192.168.101.2 and 9.24.105.171. Note that the traffic is in plaintext and Network Monitor was able to determine that this is a telnet session and gave details on the TCP header. The telnet password would clearly be seen in such a trace.

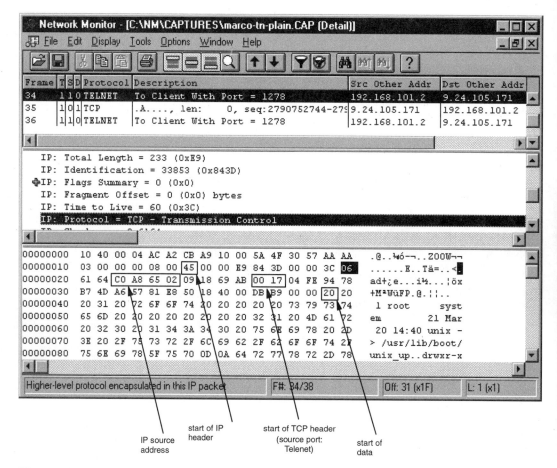

Figure 52. *Trace of a Plain TCP/IP Connection*

B.2.1.2 Example 2: AH Tunnel

We then activated an AH tunnel between the firewalls by setting the tunnel policy to auth only (see Appendix A, "IBM eNetwork VPN Solutions" on page 119), and reopened the same telnet session. Network Monitor was no longer able to analyze anything beyond the outer IP header (see Figure 53 on page 145). However, it is obvious that AH is applied; the outer IP header carries protocol number 51 (0x33). Note that the payload is in cleartext.

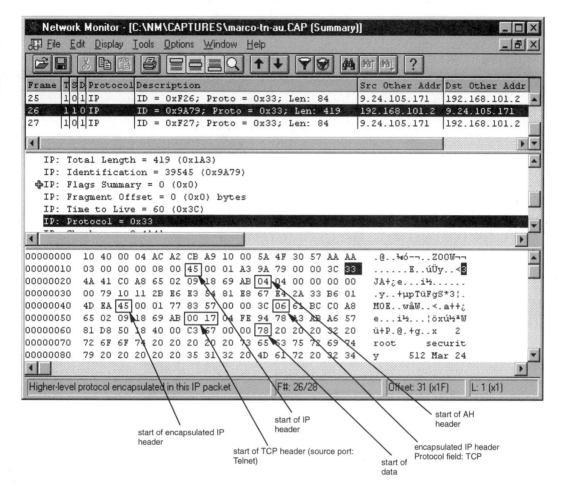

Figure 53. *Trace of an AH Tunnel*

It is not very difficult to identify the fields in the encapsulated IP packet. Have the packet format descriptions handy and consider these hints:

1. Network Monitor can highlight the outer IP header. The first byte usually has a hex value 0x45 (Version: 4, header length: five 32-bit words = 20 bytes). The 10th byte in the header indicates the protocol header that follows. This is AH (0x33) in our case.

2. Find the starting byte of the AH header. It is the first non-highlighted byte after the outer IP header (or, count a number of bytes indicated by the outer IP header length). This byte is the Next Header field; in our case IP (0x04), because AH is in tunnel mode.

3. The 2nd byte of the AH header shows its length. It is usually a 0x04 value, which means six 32-bit words = 24 bytes.

4. The four bytes starting at the 5th position contain the SPI (0x00000079). Following this things differ in function of the version of AH:

   • RFC 1826 compliant: ICV (in our case Keyed MD5, so it has 16 bytes)

   • New Draft compliant: 4 bytes of sequence number + ICV

5. After the AH header you find the encapsulated IP header. The same applies as for the outer IP header. Examining the 10th byte one can see that the next protocol header is TCP (0x06). Since the encapsulated IP header is also 20 bytes in length, the starting byte of the TCP header is quickly found. This, together with the 2nd byte show the source TCP port. It is 0x0017 = 23, the well-known telnet port. Note that you can clearly see the source and destination IP addresses in the outer as well as in the inner IP header.

6. The upper nibble of the 13th byte in the TCP header indicates its length in 32-bit words. In our case this is 0x5, which means 20 bytes. With this information the start of the data can be located.

In summary, the packet structure is the following:

Figure 54. IP Packet Inside an AH Tunnel.

B.2.1.3 Example 3: ESP Tunnel

The same setup as in the AH tunnel example before, just the tunnel has been changed to ESP (encr only policy, see Appendix A, "IBM eNetwork VPN Solutions" on page 119). Figure 55 on page 147 shows a packet from the tunnel. Note that the inner IP packet is completely garbled. Nothing besides the destination can figure out the addresses, protocols or the data carried by it. The only identifiable fields are the 32-bit SPI and the 64-bit IV in the ESP header.

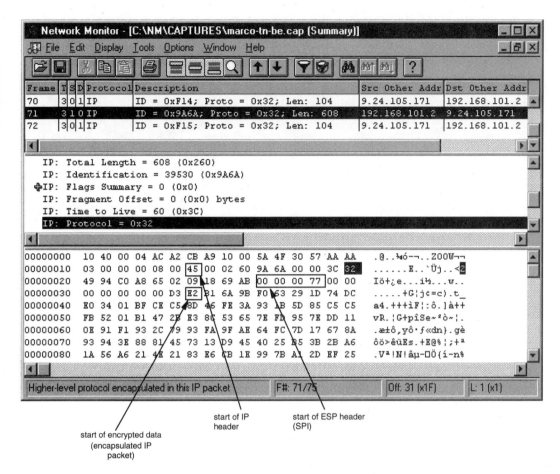

start of IP header

start of ESP header (SPI)

start of encrypted data (encapsulated IP packet)

Figure 55. *Trace of an ESP Tunnel*

Note: When ESP is applied after AH (auth/encr policy, see Appendix A, "IBM eNetwork VPN Solutions" on page 119), the trace looks exactly the same, because ESP in tunnel mode encrypts the whole original packet.

The outline of the packet is shown below. There is no ESP Authentication field, since the AIX Firewall does not yet support that feature.

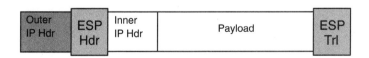

Figure 56. *IP Packet Inside an ESP Tunnel*

B.2.1.4 Example 4: Combined AH-ESP Tunnel

We modified the tunnel by setting the tunnel policy to encr/auth. The IPSec kernel first applies ESP and then AH in this case. Observe that the Next Header field in the AH header now indicates ESP (0x32). As in the previous case, we cannot examine the structure of the encapsulated IP packet.

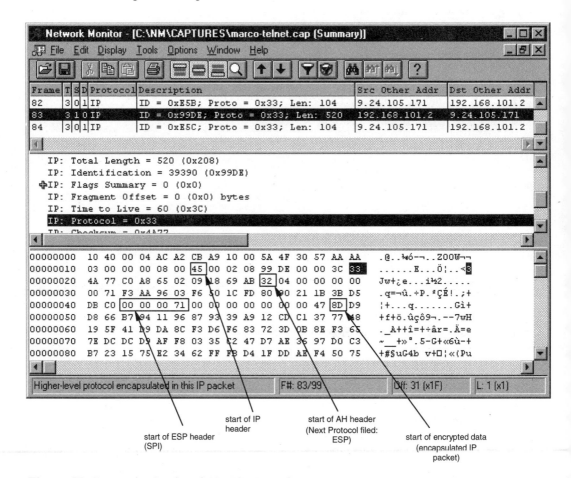

Figure 57. Trace of a Combined AH-ESP Tunnel

Given the information above, we can now draw the outline of a packet in this tunnel:

Figure 58. IP Packet Inside a Combined AH-ESP Tunnel

B.2.1.5 Example 5: Nested ESP Packet Inside AH Tunnel

This example shows a trace of the environment as described in Chapter 6, "Business Partner/Supplier Network Scenario" on page 103. The original IP datagram is first encrypted at the source host using ESP in transport mode. That datagram is then sent to the firewall where AH in tunnel mode is applied to it, thus adding an outer IP header with IP address information of the firewalls.

In contrast to the AH tunnel shown in B.2.1.2, "Example 2: AH Tunnel" on page 144, the Next Header field of the inner IP header now points to ESP instead of TCP.

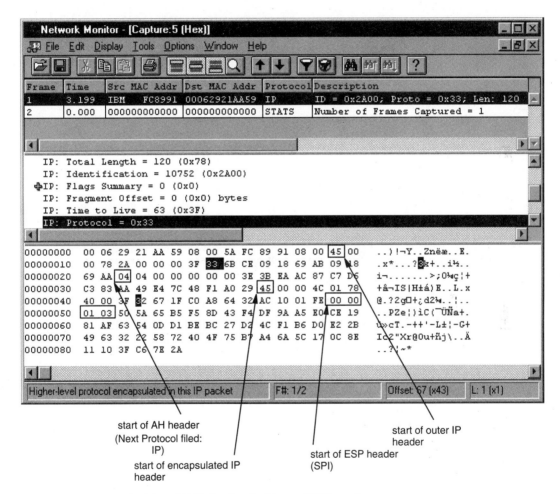

Figure 59. Trace of a Nested ESP Packet Inside an AH Tunnel

Given the information above, we can now draw the outline of a packet in this nested tunnel:

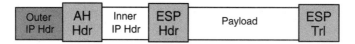

Figure 60. *ESP Packet Nested Inside an AH Tunnel*

B.3 Features That May Not Work with IPSec

There are some features present in most available TCP/IP implementations that are useful for various purposes but may not work in conjunction with IPSec. The following sections list some of them and describe the problems that can be encountered in an IPSec environment.

B.3.1 Path MTU Discovery and IP Fragmentation

When TCP calculates the maximum segment size (MSS) it doesn't know about the extra length needed for IPSec headers. MTU path discovery (described in RFC 1191) turns on the 'Do not fragement' bit in the IP header in the TCP layer. Then the IP layer calls the IPSec kernel and adds the IPSec headers. If this added length exceeds an MTU, it will be rejected because of the 'Do not fragment' bit set. So TCP will retry after reducing the MSS, but it uses the MTU returned in the ICMP response and does not take into account the IPSec header length, so the retry won't work.

When IP datagrams carrying IPSec traffic are fragmented along the way, the general rule is to apply IPSec before fragmentation for outbound datagrams, and to apply IPSec after reassembly for inbound datagrams. This must be done in order to assure proper IPSec processing for authentication and/or encryption/decryption.

See the current Internet Drafts for IPSec, AH and ESP on the issues of fragmentation and path MTU discovery.

B.3.2 Traceroute

According to the current IPSec specifications, there are certain ICMP message types that can be accepted over IPSec connections according to the local policy. You need to check with the vendor of your specific IPSec implementation if they support traceroute over IPSec.

Note: This obviously applies only to IPSec traffic in transport mode. Tunneled IPSec packets that are just passed through from one interface to another in a security gateway may carry traceroute traffic undisturbed. However, the whole purpose of traceroute is lost within IPSec tunnels because only the first gateway and the final destination, but no other intermediate gateways will respond to those packets.

B.3.3 Network Address Translation

We have described some issues with NAT and IPSec in 1.3.3.1, "Network Address Translation" on page 15. The following reference provides additional information on NAT and its implications when used in conjunction with IPSec:

```
http://www.ietf.org/internet-drafts/draft-moskowitz-net66-vpn-00.txt
```

Appendix C. Special Notices

The information in this book is not intended as the specification of any programming interfaces that are provided by any of the products discussed herein. See the PUBLICATIONS section of the IBM Programming Announcement for the discussed products for more information about what publications are considered to be product documentation.

References in this publication to IBM products, programs or services do not imply that IBM intends to make these available in all countries in which IBM operates. Any reference to an IBM product, program, or service is not intended to state or imply that only IBM's product, program, or service may be used. Any functionally equivalent program that does not infringe any of IBM's intellectual property rights may be used instead of the IBM product, program or service.

Information in this book was developed in conjunction with use of the equipment specified, and is limited in application to those specific hardware and software products and levels.

IBM may have patents or pending patent applications covering subject matter in this document. The furnishing of this document does not give you any license to these patents. You can send license inquiries, in writing, to the IBM Director of Licensing, IBM Corporation, North Castle Drive, Armonk, NY 10504-1785.

Licensees of this program who wish to have information about it for the purpose of enabling: (i) the exchange of information between independently created programs and other programs (including this one) and (ii) the mutual use of the information which has been exchanged, should contact IBM Corporation, Dept. 600A, Mail Drop 1329, Somers, NY 10589 USA.

Such information may be available, subject to appropriate terms and conditions, including in some cases, payment of a fee.

The information contained in this document has not been submitted to any formal IBM test and is distributed AS IS. The information about non-IBM ("vendor") products in this manual has been supplied by the vendor and IBM assumes no responsibility for its accuracy or completeness. The use of this information or the implementation of any of these techniques is a customer responsibility and depends on the customer's ability to evaluate and integrate them into the customer's operational environment. While each item may have been reviewed by IBM for accuracy in a specific situation, there is no guarantee that the same or similar results will be obtained elsewhere. Customers attempting to adapt these techniques to their own environments do so at their own risk.

Any pointers in this publication to external Web sites are provided for convenience only and do not in any manner serve as an endorsement of these Web sites.

Any performance data contained in this document was determined in a controlled environment, and therefore, the results that may be obtained in other operating environments may vary significantly. Users of this document should verify the applicable data for their specific environment.

The following document contains examples of data and reports used in daily business operations. To illustrate them as completely as possible, the examples contain the names of individuals, companies, brands, and products. All of these names are fictitious and any similarity to the names and addresses used by an actual business enterprise is entirely coincidental.

Reference to PTF numbers that have not been released through the normal distribution process does not imply general availability. The purpose of including these reference numbers is to alert IBM customers to specific information relative to the implementation of the PTF when it becomes available to each customer according to the normal IBM PTF distribution process.

The following terms are trademarks of the International Business Machines Corporation in the United States and/or other countries:

AIX®	AS/400®
eNetwork	IBM Global Network
IBM®	LAN Distance®
LANStreamer®	Nways
OS/2®	OS/390
OS/400®	PowerPC®
SecureWay	

The following terms are trademarks of other companies:

C-bus is a trademark of Corollary, Inc.

Java and HotJava are trademarks of Sun Microsystems, Incorporated.

Microsoft, Windows, Windows NT, and the Windows 95 logo are trademarks or registered trademarks of Microsoft Corporation.

PC Direct is a trademark of Ziff Communications Company and is used by IBM Corporation under license.

Pentium, MMX, ProShare, LANDesk, and ActionMedia are trademarks or registered trademarks of Intel Corporation in the U.S. and other countries.

UNIX is a registered trademark in the United States and other countries licensed exclusively through X/Open Company Limited.

Other company, product, and service names may be trademarks or service marks of others.

Appendix D. Related Publications

The publications listed in this section are considered particularly suitable for a more detailed discussion of the topics covered in this redbook.

D.1 International Technical Support Organization Publications

For information on ordering these ITSO publications, please refer to the ITSO home page on the World Wide Web: `http://www.redbooks.ibm.com`

- *A Comprehensive Guide to Virtual Private Networks, Volume I: IBM Firewall, Server and Client Solutions*, SG24-5201

- *Protect and Survive Using IBM Firewall 3.1 for AIX*, SG24-2577

- *Exploring the IBM eNetwork Communications Suite*, SG24-2111

- *AIX Version 4.3 Differences Guide*, SG24-2014

- *Secure Electronic Transactions: Credit Card Payment on the Web in Theory and Practice*, SG24-4978

D.2 Other Publications

These publications are also relevant as further information sources:

- *eNetwork Firewall for AIX, User*, GC31-8419

- *eNetwork Firewall for AIX, Reference Guide*, SC31-8418

- *Applied Cryptography*, second edition, John Wiley & Sons, Inc., 1996, by Bruce Schneier; ISBN 0-471-11709-9.

- *Network Security: Private Communication in a Public World*, PTR Prentice Hall, 1995, by Charlie Kaufman, Radia Perlman, and Mike Speciner; ISBN 0-13-061466-1.

- *Request For Comments (RFC)* and *Internet Drafts (ID)*

  There are more than 2300 RFCs today. For those readers who want to keep up-to-date with the latest advances and research activities in TCP/IP, the ever-increasing number of RFCs and Internet Drafts (ID) is the best source of this information. RFCs can be viewed or obtained online from the Internet

Engineering Taskforce (IETF) Web page using the following URL:
`http://www.ietf.org.`

D.2.1 Web Site Reference

The following is a list of World Wide Web sites that we also consider as relevant sources of further information:

Current IPSec Internet Drafts (see3.5, "Current IPSec Standards and Internet Drafts" on page 68 for a detailed list of the core IPSec specifications)
>`http://www.ietf.org/ids.by.wg/ipsec.html`

IBM eNetwork home page
>`http://www.software.ibm.com/enetwork`

IBM eNetwork Firewall home page
>`http://www.software.ibm.com/enetwork/firewall`

IBM eNetwork Virtual Private Networks home page
>`http://www.software.ibm.com/enetwork/technology/vpn/`

IBM AIX home page
>`http://www.rs6000.ibm.com/software/aix_os.html`

IBM OS/390 IPSec information
>`http://www.s390.ibm.com/products/mvs/firewall/ipsec.htm`

IBM Software Choice home page (TCP/IP V4.1 for OS/2 and prerequisites)
>`http://service.software.ibm.com/asd-bin/doc/index.htm`

IBM Corp. home page
>`http://www.ibm.com`

FTP Software, Inc., home page
>`http://www.ftp.com`

SSL Information
>`http://home.netscape.com/assist/security/ssl/index.html`

U.S. version of Pretty Good Privacy (PGP)
>`http://www.pgp.com.`

International version of Pretty Good Privacy (PGP)
>`http://www.pgpi.com.`

List of Abbreviations

AH	Authentication Header	*DHCP*	Dynamic Host Configuration Protocol
AIX	Advanced Interactive Executive	*DLL*	Dynamic Link Library
API	Application Programming Interface	*DNS*	Domain Name Server
ARP	Address Resolution Protocol	*DOI*	Domain of Interpretation
		DOS	Disk Operating System
ASCII	American Standard Code for Information Interchange	*DSA*	Digital Signature Algorithm
		DSS	Digital Signature Standard
AS/400	Application System/400	*EBCDIC*	Extended Binary Communication Data Interchange Code
ATM	Asynchronous Transfer Mode		
CA	Certification Authority	*ESP*	Encapsulating Security Payload
CBC	Cipher Block Chaining	*FTP*	File Transfer Protocol
CHAP	Challenge Handshake Authentication Protocol	*GUI*	Graphical User Interface
		HMAC	Hashed Message Authentication Code
CPU	Central Processing Unit		
CDMF	Commercial Data Masking Facility	*HTML*	Hypertext Markup Language
DDNS	Dynamic Domain Name System	*HTTP*	Hypertext Transfer Protocol
DES	Digital Encryption Standard	*IAB*	Internet Activities Board

IANA	Internet Assigned Numbers Authority	*ISAKMP*	Internet Security Association and Key Management Protocol
IBM	International Business Machines Corporation	*ISDN*	Integrated Services Digital Network
ICMP	Internet Control Message Protocol	*ISO*	International Organization for Standardization
ICSS	Internet Connection Secure Server	*ISP*	Internet Service Provider
ICV	Integrity Check Value	*ITSO*	International Technical Support Organization
IDEA	International Data Encryption Algorithm	*IV*	Initialization Vector
IEEE	Institute of Electrical and Electronics Engineers	*LAN*	Local Area Network
IESG	Internet Engineering Steering Group	*LDAP*	Lightweight Directory Access Protocol
IETF	Internet Engineering Task Force	*LLC*	Logical Link Layer
IGMP	Internet Group Management Protocol	*L2TP*	Layer 2 Tunneling Protocol
IGN	IBM Global Network	*MAC*	Message Authentication Code
IKE	Internet Key Exchange	*MAC*	Media Access Control
IP	Internet Protocol	*MD2*	RSA Message Digest 2 Algorithm
IPC	Interprocess Communication	*MD5*	RSA Message Digest 5 Algorithm
IPSec	IP Security Architecture		

MIB	Management Information Base	*NVT*	Network Virtual Terminal
MIME	Multipurpose Internet Mail Extensions	*OSPF*	Open Shortest Path First
MPTN	Multiprotocol Transport Network	*OS/2*	Operating System/2
MS-CHAP	Microsoft Challenge Handshake Authentication Protocol	*PAP*	Password Authentication Protocol
		PGP	Pretty Good Privacy
		POP	Post Office Protocol
MVS	Multiple Virtual Storage Operating System	*PPP*	Point-to-Point Protocol
NAT	Network Address Translation	*PPTP*	Point-to-Point Tunneling Protocol
NDIS	Network Device Interface Specification	*PSTN*	Public Switched Telephone Network
NFS	Network File System	*QOS*	Quality of Service
NIC	Network Information Center	*RAM*	Random Access Memory
		RARP	Reverse Address Resolution Protocol
NIS	Network Information Systems	*RAS*	Remote Access Service
NIST	National Institute of Standards and Technology	*RC4*	RSA Rivest Cipher 4 Algorithm
NNTP	Network News Transfer Protocol	*RFC*	Request for Comments
NSA	National Security Agency	*RISC*	Reduced Instruction Set Computer
NTP	Network Time Protocol		

RIP	Routing Information Protocol	**SOCKS**	SOCK-et-S: An internal NEC development name that remained after release
ROM	Read-only Memory		
RSH	Remote Shell	**SPI**	Security Parameter Index
RS/6000	IBM RISC System/6000		
SA	Security Association	**SSL**	Secure Sockets Layer
SET	Secure Electronic Transactions	**TCP**	Transmission Control Protocol
S-HTTP	Secure Hypertext Transfer Protocol	**TCP/IP**	Transmission Control Protocol / Internet Protocol
SLIP	Serial Line Internet Protocol	**TOS**	Type of Service
S-MIME	Secure Multipurpose Internet Mail Extension	**TTL**	Time to Live
		UDP	User Datagram Protocol
SMIT	System Management Interface Tool	**URL**	Uniform Resource Locator
SMTP	Simple Mail Transfer Protocol	**VPN**	Virtual Private Network
SNG	Secured Network Gateway (former product name of the AIX firewall)	**WAN**	Wide Area Network
		WWW	World Wide Web
SNMP	Simple Network Management Protocol	**3DES**	Triple Digital Encryption Standard

Index

Special Characters

/etc/security/fwfilters.cfg file 141

Numerics

2210/2216 Router
   3DES 132
   auth policy 132
   auth/encr policy 132
   CDMF 132
   DES CBC 8 132
   encr policy 132
   encr/auth policy 132
   HMAC MD5 132
   HMAC SHA 132
   layer 2 tunneling 119
   logging 132
   manual tunnel 121, 132
   MAS V3.1 132
   MRS V3.1 132
   Multiprotocol Routing Services
     V3.1 132
   multiprotocol support 119
   Nways Multiprotocol Access Services
     V3.1 132
   packet filtering 132
   transport mode 132
   tunnel mode 132
3746 Multiaccess Enclosure 126
3DES 132, 134
3DES CBC 120, 129
509 43

A

A5 algorithm 30
abbreviations 159

access control 17, 105, 108
access control policy 7
ACE/SecurID cards 137
acronyms 159
address spoofing 90
AH
   See Authentication Header (AH)
AIX V4.3
   3DES CBC 129
   auth policy 129
   auth/encr policy 129
   authentication algorithm 130
   CDMF 129
   DES CBC 4 129
   DES CBC 8 129
   encr policy 129, 130
   encr/auth policy 129, 130
   filter rules 130
   HMAC MD5 129
   HMAC SHA 129
   host-firewall-host option 131
   IBM tunnel 123, 129
   ipreport command 142
   iptrace command 142
   IPv6 132
   IPv6) 130
   keyed MD5 129
   logging 130, 132
   manual tunnel 121, 129
   packet filtering 130
   SMIT IPSec panels 130, 131
   transport mode 129
   triple DES 132
   tunnel definition 130
   tunnel ID 131
   tunnel mode 129
algorithm, block 29

algorithm, key-exchange   33
algorithm, public-key   33
algorithm, RSA   34
algorithm, stream   29
algorithm, symmetric   29, 30
algorithms, public-key   32
application gateways   18
application layer security   20
arithmetic, modular   34
Assigned Numbers RFC   52
asymmetric algorithm   34
auth only policy   119
auth policy   128, 129, 132, 133, 138, 139, 144
auth/encr policy   120, 128, 129, 132, 133, 138, 147
authentication   27, 29, 32, 37, 38, 90, 105, 106, 108, 110, 112, 119, 120
authentication algorithm   120, 130
Authentication Header (AH)
   AH   90, 98, 105, 106, 116, 119, 128, 129, 132, 133, 138, 139, 142
   authentication   92, 94, 112, 120
   Authentication Data   53
   Authentication Data field   39
   checksum   10
   combinations with ESP   62
   data integrity   10
   data origin authentication   10
   Flags field   51
   Fragment Offset   51
   header checksum   51
   header format   52
   HMAC MD5   120, 129, 132, 139
   HMAC SHA   120, 129, 132
   HMAC MD5-96   53
   HMAC-SHA-1-96   53
   ICV   146
   integrity check value   16
   Integrity Check Value (ICV)   53
   IP fragment   51
   IPv6 environment   56

Authentication Header (AH) *(continued)*
   Keyed MD5   53, 120, 128, 129, 133, 138, 139
   message authentication code   10
   mutable fields   51, 54
   Next Header field   52, 145, 148
   Payload Length   52
   protocol number   142, 144
   replay protection   10, 53, 120
   Reserved field   52
   secret shared key   11
   Security Parameter Index (SPI)   53
   Sequence Number   53
   sequence number field   11
   Time To Live (TTL)   51
   transform   47
   transport mode   53, 64
   tunnel mode   53, 64, 90, 92, 105, 106, 149
   Type of Service (TOS)   51
authentication method   76
automatic key refresh   99

B

bibliography   157
block algorithm   29
brute-force attack   30
bulk encryption   33

C

CBC   29
CDMF   30, 120, 122, 128, 129, 132, 133, 138
certificate   73
certificate authority   80
Certificate Management   15
certification authority (CA)   43
cipher   28
Cipher Block Chaining (CBC)   29
cipher, restricted   28

internal segment 3
International Data Encryption Algorithm
(IDEA) 30
Internet Assigned Numbers Authority
(IANA) 52
Internet Connection Secure Server
(ICSS) 109
Internet Draft 47, 62, 119
Internet Engineering Steering Group
(IESG) 16
Internet Engineering Task Force (IETF) 2,
5
Internet Key Exchange (IKE)
  See ISAKMP/Oakley
Internet Security Association and Key
  Management Protocol (ISAKMP)
  See ISAKMP/Oakley
IP routing protocol 91
IP Security Architecture (IPSec)
  3DES CBC 120
  asymmetric algorithm 34
  authentication 39, 106, 120
  Authentication Header (AH)
    See Authentication Header (AH)
  authentication protocols 90
  automated management 10
  CDMF 30, 120
  combinations of AH and ESP 62
  combined tunnel 65
  concepts 47
  cryptographic concepts 27
  cryptographic keys 10
  data confidentiality 10
  data integrity 10
  data origin authentication 10
  DES 30
  DES CBC 4 120
  DES CBC 8 120
  Diffie-Hellman algorithm 35
  Diffie-Hellman key exchange 35
  digital certificate 44
  digital signature 44

IP Security Architecture (IPSec) *(continued)*
  Digital Signature Algorithm 41
  Encapsulating Security Payload (ESP)
    See Encapsulating Security Payload
    (ESP)
  encapsulation 49
  encryption: 120
  Hashed Message Authentication Code
    (HMAC) 40
  HMAC 40, 90
  HMAC MD5 120
  HMAC SHA 120
  HMAC-MD5-96 39
  HMAC-SHA-1-96 39
  IBM 2210 14
  IBM 2216 15
  IDEA 30
  initialization vector 45
  integrity 39
  Internet Security Association and Key
    Management Protocol (ISAKMP)
    See ISAKMP/Oakley
  IPSec Bakeoffs 140
  IPSec device drivers 138
  IPSec kernel 18, 96, 97, 98, 116, 117,
    122, 138, 142, 150
  IPSec module 48
  IPSec policies 49
  IPSec standards 140
  IPSec tunnel 50
  IPSec Working Group 140
  iterated tunneling 63
  kernel modules 125
  key distribution 109
  key management 108
  Keyed MD5 39, 120
  Keyed SHA-1 39
  manual key distribution 108
  modulus 34, 35
  nested tunneling 63
  nested tunnels 142
  nesting of IPSec protocols 107

ISAKMP/Oakley *(continued)*
    identity payload 79, 80, 81
    Identity Protect exchange 74
    Initiator Cookie 75, 76, 78
    Integrity Check Value (ICV) 86
    ISAKMP Header 75, 76, 80, 82, 84, 86
    Key Exchange attribute 82
    Key Exchange field 78, 83
    Key Exchange Payload 85
    KEY_OAKLEY 76, 77
    keying material 72, 78, 79, 85, 87
    LDAP 80
    man-in-the-middle 72
    master key 74
    master secret 73
    Message 1 75, 83, 87
    Message 2 76, 85, 87
    Message 3 77, 86
    Message 4 78
    Message 5 79
    Message 6 81
    Message ID 75, 76, 85, 86
    Message ID field 82
    Message-ID 84
    nonce 77, 78, 83, 85
    Nonce field 78
    Nonce Payload 85
    nonce: 85
    nonces 87
    Oakley Main Mode 74, 82
    Oakley Quick Mode 82
    oPFS 72
    Perfect Forward Secrecy (PFS) 72, 82
    permanent identifier 73, 88
    PFS 82
    Phase 1 73
    Phase 2 73
    pre-shared keys 72
    private value 77, 78
    Proposal Payload 75, 76, 84
    protection suite 87
    Protection Suites 75

ISAKMP/Oakley *(continued)*
    PROTO_ISAKMP 75, 76
    protocol code point 85
    proxy negotiator 83
    pseudo-random function 76, 84
    public key 73
    public value 77, 78, 81, 83, 84, 85, 87
    remote access 88
    remote host 73, 88
    Responder Cookie 75, 76, 78
    revised RSA public key
      authentication 77
    RSA 44
    RSA algorithm 34
    RSA public key authentication 77
    RSA public key encryption 72
    secure DNS server 80
    secure local cache 80
    security association 11, 73, 74, 77, 81,
      82
    Security Association field 75, 76
    Security Association Payload 84, 87
    Security Payload 85
    security protection suite 73
    signature payload 79
    SKEYID 74, 78, 81, 85
    SKEYID_a 79, 84
    SKEYID_d 79
    SKEYID_e 79
    SPI 80, 85, 87, 88
    Transform Payload 76, 77, 84
ISP 66, 89, 113
ISP access box 3, 5
iterated tunneling 63
IV 29

K

kernel modules 125
key distribution 109
key generation 45

random-number generator 44, 45
RC2 46
RC4 46
refresh keys 82
remote access 88
remote client 115
remote host 5, 12, 67, 73
remote user 4, 24, 111
replay prevention 122, 129
replay protection 53, 120
restricted cipher 28
RFC 1826 53
RFC 1827 58
router 50
routing algorithms 93
routing collisions 104
routing domains 5
routing extension header 56, 61
routing protocol 107
RSA 33
RSA algorithm 34
RSA encryption standard
    See IP Security Architecture (IPSec)

S

SA bundle 48, 65, 106
SA type 121
secret, shared 33
secure DNS server 80
Secure Electronic Transaction (SET) 38
Secure Hash Algorithm 1 (SHA-1) 39
Secure HTTP (S-HTTP) 19
secure interface 97, 99, 116
Secure Internet Mail Extension
  (S-MIME) 9
secure local cache 80
Secure Multipurpose Internet Mail Extension
  (S-MIME) 19
secure network 96, 100, 102
Secure Sockets Layer 9, 15, 19, 109, 124,
 137

Secured Network Gateway (SNG)
  V2.2 128
security association 90, 94, 97, 98, 105,
  106, 108, 121
Security Association Database (SAD) 49
security exposures 8
security gateway 3, 5, 7, 50, 89
security parameter index 121
Security Parameter Index (SPI) 48, 53, 58
Security Policy Database (SPD) 48
selectors 50
sequence numbers 32
service (firewall) 95
session key lifetime 109, 122, 123
session key refresh time 123
SET 38, 44
SHA-1 39
SHA-1, Keyed 39
shared keys 33
shared secret 33, 36, 39, 40
SKEYID 78, 85
SKEYID_a 79, 84
SKEYID_d 79
SKEYID_e 79
SMIT IPSec panels 130, 131
SNG 128
SOCKS 9, 18, 89
socksified applications 18
source address 17
SPI 121, 122, 123, 129, 139
spoofing attack 13, 17, 20
SSL 109, 124, 137
SSL control session 114, 117, 124
stateful inspection 17
stateless inspection 17
static filter rules 111
stream algorithm 29
strong cryptography 27, 62
symmetric algorithm 29, 30

T

target user   124, 125
TCP header   107
TCP/IP V4.1 for OS/2   138
Time To Live (TTL)   51
timestamp   32
transform   47
transport adjacency   63, 65
transport mode   106, 121, 129, 132, 139,
  149
triple DES   132
triple-DES   30, 45
trust chain   43
tunnel   50
  dynamic tunnel   99, 113, 117, 124, 128,
    138
  IBM tunnel   123, 124, 127, 128, 129,
    134
  IPSec tunnel   50
  L2TP tunnel   13
  manual tunnel   99, 108, 114, 121, 123,
    125, 128, 129, 132, 133, 138, 139
  transport mode   138
  tunnel definition   129, 130
  tunnel endpoint   96
  tunnel ID   95, 97, 98, 116, 117, 122,
    131, 141
  tunnel management   111
  tunnel mode   97, 98, 105, 106, 121, 128,
    129, 132, 133, 138, 139, 149
  tunnel owner   133
  tunnel parameters   111
  tunnel partner   133
  tunnel policy   119
  tunnel type   113
  tunneling protocol   6
tunneling   49
Type of Service (TOS)   51

V

value, hash   39
virtual private network
  business scenarios   20
  certificate management   24
  data link layer-based   8
  end-to-end security   3
  IPSec-based   8
  layer 2-based   8
  network layer-based   8
  policy directory   15
  policy management   24
  secure domain name server   24
  security policy   22
  vendors   12
VPN
  See virtual private network

X

X.509 certificates   19